COGNITIVE-BEHAVIORAL THERAPY

(CBT) TECHNIQUES TO OVERCOME ANXIETY, REMOVE DEPRESSION AND NEGATIVITY FROM YOUR BRAIN, A BEGINNER GUIDE MADE SIMPLE TO RETRAINING YOUR EMPATH IN PLAIN ENGLISH.

Table of Contents

Introduction

Cognitive behavioral therapy (CBT) is a form of psychotherapy that solves an individual's problems by helping them modify both their thoughts and actions. CBT takes on a practical approach toward solving problems. Its goal is to remedy toxic thought-patterns and behaviors that have contributed to a person's distress and thus restore happiness. CBT is commonly used in treating a number of problems, such as relationship issues, sleeping difficulties, drug abuse, anxiety, and depression.

One of the biggest advantages of CBT is its shortness. It takes about six to ten months for the treatment of most emotional problems. Clients attend weekly sessions or a session every two weeks, with each session lasting about an hour. During the session, the client bares their soul, and the therapist comes up with the strategies of solving the problem. The therapist introduces a set of principles to the patient. And these lifelong principles are to help the patient overcome their problems.

Psychologists consider CBT to be a blend of psychotherapy and behavioral therapy. Psychotherapy highlights the value of the personal meanings we ascribe to things and how thinking patterns start in early childhood. Behavioral therapy explores the connection between our challenges, behaviors, and thoughts. To achieve maximum results, psychotherapists must tailor CBT to the precise needs and character of every patient.

The History of Cognitive Behavioral Therapy

Aaron Beck, a psychiatrist, is the man that came up with cognitive behavioral therapy in the 1960s. During psychoanalysis, Aaron realized that some of his patients appeared to talk to themselves, a sign of internal dialogue, but the patients only reported a small part of these thoughts to him.

For instance, during therapy, the patient might think to herself, The therapist seems a bit cold today. Have I done something to annoy him? Such a line of thought could make the patient anxious. But then the patient says to herself, Maybe he's tired, or he had a terrible encounter with someone before coming here. The second thought would potentially make the patient go from anxious to comfortable and well-adjusted. Thus, by changing their thoughts, they get to change their feelings.

Aaron Beck found out that the connection between thoughts and feelings was crucial. He said that people weren't always conscious of their emotion-filled thoughts, but they could be trained to recognize them. Beck thought that it was necessary for a person to identify their emotion-filled thoughts in order to remedy their problems.

The Place of Negative Thoughts

According to CBT, whatever happens to us is not liable for our frustrations, but the meaning that we ascribe to it. If something terrible goes down, it is the accompanying negative thoughts that will make us feel terrible, not the deed itself.

For example, if a woman is suffering from depression, she might think to herself, If I go to work today, I'll botch things up. I feel horrible. Because of believing her negative thoughts, she is going to call in sick and miss work. She's the victim of her thoughts – not her depression. She made an incorrect assumption. Maybe if she'd gone to work, she'd have found something to do and proceeded to be extremely productive. However, sitting at home for the whole day, the negativity increases tenfold, and she's thinking, Oh, I'm such a letdown! Where do I go from here? The woman ends up feeling even worse than before. Her emotion-filled thoughts place her in a vicious cycle that sends her spiraling down into a continuously worse state.

Where Do These Negative Thoughts Come From?

According to Aaron Beck, the most negative thinking patterns are rooted in our childhood experiences. A child who never received parental love might grow up to want validation from the external world. For this, they will strive to do something extraordinary to capture everyone's attention and bask in the validation that they will earn. But this might place the person in a situation known as a dysfunctional assumption. This is where a previously unloved person assumes that they always have to do something great in order to be loved by people, and this notion makes them pursue success relentlessly, yet when they experience failure, the dysfunctional assumption is activated, and they start perceiving themselves as failures who will never recover.

Cognitive behavioral therapy is geared at helping patients understand the role of their negative thoughts in their distressing lives. Patients can recognize their automatic thoughts and test their validity. For instance, in the case of the depressed woman, instead of thinking at once that she won't cope at work, she should have prodded for reasons that support the opposite.

CBT Treatment

The difference between cognitive behavioral therapy and other forms of psychotherapies is that CBT sessions are structured, and purposely discourage patients from having a multidimensional talk. At the start, the patient meets the therapist to divulge their specific challenges. The therapist sets goals that the patient must achieve within a certain time frame. The problems are varied in nature: sleeping troubles, difficulties in socializing, lack of concentration, or even unhappy marriage.

The challenges and the goals form the basis of the session structures. During each session, the therapist and the patient will jointly agree on the milestone they have to reach. The sessions have to be structured in a progressive way, with the easy parts tackled before the difficult ones. At the end of each session, there has to be an assignment to be performed before the next session.

Who Can Be Helped By CBT?

CBT is most effective when there are clear goals. For this reason, people with specific challenges are the most suitable for CBT treatment. People with vague feelings and who have no particular aspect of their lives that they want to develop will not achieve great results with CBT.

CBT can help solve the following issues:

- Anger issues

- Anxiety
- Panic attacks

- Chronic fatigue syndrome

- Chronic pain

- Depression
- Alcoholism
- Bulimia nervosa

- Mood swings

- Obsessive-compulsive disorder

- Phobias
- Insomnia

Chapter 1 A Step-By-Step Guide To Cbt

Cognitive behavioral therapy helps to alleviate various problems by providing a short, goal-oriented, and problem-specific approach. The success of CBT hinges upon the active involvement of the patient. The therapist and the patient jointly write down the goals that they should achieve within a certain time frame. In the beginning, the patient must work alongside the therapist, but ultimately, the patient could become their own therapist.

- First off, the patient must scout for a therapist that they are comfortable working with.

- If the patient lucks out to find the best therapist, an appointment is set up.

- During the first appointment, the patient will divulge every last detail about their problems, with the therapist asking necessary questions.

- The therapist is to draft a set of milestones to be achieved within a certain amount of time.

- Then the therapist will come up with a structured CBT course that will help the patient realize the set milestones.

- The patient is expected to attend sessions over the next few months until they achieve their goals.

Beliefs that CBT is based upon

- Unhelpful ways that people think can lead to mental and emotional problems: At the root of our challenges, is a complex web of unhelpful thoughts. These negative thinking patterns not only hinder us from having clarity of thought but also give way to harmful behaviors. For instance, if a college student becomes a young mother, it is so easy for her to abandon the dreams she had and focus on being a mother. However, if she can view her condition from the angle of positivity, she will continue pursuing her goals despite the fact that she has a child.

- If people learn toxic behaviors, this too can lead to mental and emotional problems: For the most part, a toxic behavior is acquired from negative associations. If a young man starts hanging out with the wrong crowd, he will become influenced negatively. The crowd might make him smoke cigarettes, consume alcohol, and get involved in reckless sexual behavior. These kinds of behaviors would erode his sense of morality and convert him into a decadent young man. Toxic behaviors are like cancer – they spread out to all the parts. Thus, the person will start having troubles in his relationships, finances, spirituality, and work environment.

- People can learn more helpful ways of thinking and behaving: It's all about awareness and making a commitment. The helpful ways of thinking and behaving are not alien to us. We have many models that we can cope from. If we apply ourselves, we can modify both our thoughts and behaviors. Learning great behaviors is about consuming the right information and keeping the right associations. Ensure that you keep company with positive people so that you may copy their positivity. Also, ensure that you feed your mind with positivity, so that your emotions may stabilize.

- Fresh habits can allay symptoms of mental and physical conditions and allow people to behave in better ways: Innovation is at the heart of the advancement of a human being. When you create new routines and take on new habits, you reduce the potency of your mental and physical issues and increase your capacity to be more grounded. You acquire new habits by being an interesting person and developing your strengths. If you focus on improving your skills and capabilities, you stimulate your creative mind in the process. This is likely to lead you into new habits that you never thought possible.

The therapist and the patient must work together in order to reach the set milestones.

CBT can help the Patient Learn the Following:

- Identify problems more clearly: Through the various principles set down by the therapist, a patient is in a position to understand the true nature of their problems. Some feelings may have a sense of ambiguity so that the problem becomes two-faced. But CBT helps you understand precisely what ails you and how you can restore your health.

- Become aware of automatic thoughts: Aaron Beck argued that automatic thoughts influence most of our thinking patterns and behaviors. These automatic thoughts are basically emotion-filled thoughts. They are rooted in our early childhood, and it is difficult to be conscious of them. Recognizing automatic thoughts is a big step toward solving your problems.

- Challenge untrue assumptions: For most people battling mental health issues, holding untrue assumptions is the norm. For instance, they might think that no one loves them, they are ugly, or they are not good enough. All of these assumptions can be challenged and proven to be erroneous. This helps them get started on the path to recovery.

- Differentiate facts from myths: We live in an era where myths tend to be perpetuated at the expense of facts. This causes people to be extremely sensitive to their plight. However, through CBT, a person can tell apart the truth from deception. This empowers them to make appropriate decisions.

- Understand how the past affects the present: If you had a nasty childhood experience, it most likely scarred you and the effects are noticeable to this day. For instance, you may be prone to catching panic attacks or developing anxiety whenever your mind calls back the memories of your early childhood.

The Advantages of CBT

CBT has been proven to be extremely effective in the treatment of stress-related conditions and anxiety. The following are some of the advantages of CBT:

- Time-saving: CBT doesn't take long to complete as compared to other talk therapies. People with mental and emotional ailments favor taking CBT because it is both short and effective. As long as the therapist and the patient get along, then it becomes easy to reach the set milestones.

- Focuses on modifying your thoughts and behaviors: The main philosophy of CBT is that a person's thought patterns and behaviors are responsible for their feelings. So CBT takes on a practical approach to modify the thoughts and behaviors of a person, and, as a result, improve their feelings.

CBT principles are very useful: The set of principles and skills that a therapist hands down to the patient are extremely helpful in day-to-day living. They can be applied in every phase of life. These skills help a person to become all-around developed and better at overcoming various life difficulties.

Chapter 2 All About CBT

Originally developed as a means of helping those who are dealing with depression, Cognitive Behavioral Therapy, or CBT, is a type of psychotherapy that has proved extremely successful, so much so, that its usage has been expanded to treat additional mental health issues including many types of anxiety disorders and the fear associated with extreme phobias. Essentially, the goal of CBT is to help patients control their personal issues by first changing the thoughts that cause the issues in the first place.

CBT utilizes aspects of behavior therapy as well as cognitive therapy and posits the idea that not all behaviors can be controlled with conscious thought alone. As such, there are many different types of behaviors that are built layer upon layer over time through a mix of long-term conditioning as well as internal and external stimuli. This means that CBT differs from many types of therapy in that it doesn't worry about the hidden meanings behind the things you do and the thoughts you think; instead, it focuses on doing what needs to be done to get the results you are looking for. As such, it tends to be the most effective for those who come to it with a specific problem they are looking to solve rather than a general desire for therapy.

This, in turn, will make it easier for the CBT-trained therapist you choose to figure out the best course of action for you moving forward. Issues including depression are considered to be a mixture of harmful stimuli and an equally harmful fear avoidance response. Issues that CBT is known to positively affect include psychotic disorders, dependence, nervous tics, addiction, eating disorders, personality disorders, anxiety disorders and mood swings. While CBT isn't for everyone, it is known to present a marked improvement over some other forms of therapy including psychodynamic options. Really, when it comes down to it, whatever works best for you is the best type of therapy. Ask a mental health care professional if CBT might be right for you.

A significant part of CBT has to do with the spotting and analyzing of what are known as cognitive distortions. First popularized by a pair of scientists named Kanfer and Saslow, the idea of cognitive distortions is now used by both therapists and computer programs as a means of shining a light on the many common, yet thoroughly inaccurate beliefs that people—and machines—are prone to make on a regular basis. This includes things like jumping to negative conclusions, minimizing the impact of positives, putting too much emphasis on the negatives, and applying results from isolated incidents to a wide variety of scenarios.

Many of these distortions are based on over-generalizations of one type or another, often associated with sometime of discriminatory thought or false belief. CBT is especially useful in allowing those who follow through with treatments to become more aware and mindful of the limits their distortions place on them in an effort to minimize the effects of the same. Every person's psyche is going to be made up of a mixture of learned behaviors, if-then statements, and assumed emotions, not to mention the coping skills that were learned to force everything else to work together as best as possible. When you factor in the fact that any one of these could be warped in such a way that it has led to a negative adaptation, it becomes easier to understand the work CBT has cut out for it. Ideally, however, it will take these distortions and replace them with positive alternatives instead.

CBT History

Some exercises used in CBT have been in semi-regular use for thousands of years, such as the first recorded use among the Stoic philosophers in ancient Greece. They understood that logic was extremely useful when it came to determining which beliefs are true and which are false, and that understanding the difference was crucial to living an efficient and happy life. This idea is still one that drives modern CBT practitioners when they seek out issues that present themselves as negative thoughts and actions.

Cognitive therapy and behavioral therapy: Modern CBT can trace its roots back to behavioral therapy, which gained popularity in the 1920s thanks to the famous Pavlov's dogs experiment. This led to the idea that automatic behaviors can be trained based on external stimuli and was adapted for therapy by 1924 when a scientist named Mary Cover Jones started using it to help children deal with particularly robust fears. Behavioral therapy continued to gain acceptance throughout the 30s and 40s, and by the 1950s, it was one of the main types of therapies used to help individuals with these types of issues.

Meanwhile, in the early 1960s, a therapist by the name of Aaron T. Beck was working with associative therapy when he had a breakthrough about the nature of thought. Specifically, he realized that all thoughts are not formed unconsciously, which gives some the power to generate real, emotional responses as a result. This led to the creation of cognitive therapy in an effort to learn more about automatic thoughts.

Coming together: While behavioral therapy is great for numerous specific neurotic disorders, it isn't especially helpful in allowing patients to deal with their depression successfully. As such, by the 1960s, it had begun to be used less frequently, even as cognitive therapy really began to gain popularity. However, both types of therapy were already focusing on similar behavioral aspects to their treatment programs and also tended to focus more exclusively on what was going on in the present rather than other popular forms of therapy. Eventually, tests were conducted to see just where the differences between the two started and stopped, and after that, a mixture of the two slowly became the norm. However, the two were inexorably linked when two therapists, Dr. Clark and Dr. Barlow, used a combination approach to develop an extremely successful treatment for panic disorders.

CBT assessment

The goal of CBT has never been to catalog every single issue that a particular patient is dealing with in an effort to determine what type of officially sanctioned mental health issue they are dealing with. Rather, it is much more interested in looking at the bigger picture in order to determine the true root of the problem. The goal then can either be to reevaluate how you deal with certain situations and then respond to negative thinking, or possibly change the way you naturally view different types of situations overall in hopes of mitigating trigger behaviors or negative habits.

The average cognitive behavioral assessment is made up of five different steps.

- Picking out primary behaviors

- Analyzing said behaviors

- Looking more closely at negative behaviors in an effort to determine their overall intensity, how long they last, and how frequently they occur.

- Decide on the best way to correct said behaviors

- Decide how effective the treatment is likely to be.

Stages of CBT

Therapeutic alliance: The therapists who work patients through a round of CBT treatment don't work with clients so much as they form what are known as therapeutic alliances with them. As such, instead of listening to their client's problems and making a diagnosis, the CBT therapist works with the patient to come up with solutions that make sense to both parties to deal with the problems that are presented as a normal part of the therapy. This isn't going to happen immediately, however; the first thing that is going to happen is a session where patient and therapist get to know one another in an effort to determine if they are likely to work well together.

During initial sessions, the therapist will also assess the patient's mental and physical states in order to more quickly get to the root of the current problems. The goal for the end of the first session should be for both parties to determine if they can create a positive working relationship to effectively deal with the issues in question. This alliance is a crucial part of a successful CBT experience which means that the patient needs to take a serious look at how they feel about the therapist to ensure that they are comfortable opening up to them as this is the only way that true change can occur.

If you are starting a CBT therapy session and do not feel comfortable with the therapist that you have chosen, it is important to break off the new relationship and find someone that you do feel comfortable with. CBT is all about building positive habits to replace the negative and stifling ones, and this can't be done if you can't think of you and your therapist being on the same team. If something about the situation seems as though it is not working out, don't be afraid to go back to the drawing board and try something else instead; the therapist may even be able to give you alternative suggestions.

Control your thought process: After you have successfully formed a therapeutic alliance with a therapist you are comfortable with and have determined which problems you are going to be focusing on, you will start working on numerous different ways to control your own thought processes. In order to do so, you will need to understand what causes you to think the way you do. As such, the early sessions you attend will likely include some delving into your past to determine how, if at all, it actually relates to the problems you are currently experiencing.

Individual thoughts and patterns that were created as a way of coping with things that you had to deal with in the past are known as schemas, and getting rid of the negative ones that are preventing you from reaching your full potential is crucial in maximizing your long-term success. Part of this process will involve coming to terms with your preconceptions, which means analyzing how you think about certain things and exploring the reasons why this might be the case. During this stage, it is also normal for the patient to receive homework in the form of different exercises that you need to practice in order to start reliably changing negative thoughts and actions. While this portion of the treatment officially has no set length of time, an entire CBT treatment program rarely takes more than sixteen weeks to complete.

Practice: Once you have a better understanding of the way that you think, you and your therapist will then begin looking more closely at the way your thoughts and actions interact with one another in order to create the types of patterns that promote positive, rather than negative, behavior. Practice is the name of the game during this stage, as only practicing them on a regular basis will aid you in replacing your negative habits with positive alternatives. You and your therapist will also discuss new exercises during this stage, exercises specifically designed to replace negative patterns with improved versions. The end goal for this stage is for you finally gain control over your actions.

Final stage: You will be ready to enter the final stage of CBT when you feel confident that you can successfully manage your personal issues without your therapist's help. This doesn't mean that you will want to stop your treatment, however; instead, it will mean taking on the responsibility of managing your exercises on your own and keeping yourself inline when it comes to keeping up with the structure you will have recently grown accustomed to. Unlike many other types of therapy, it is entirely possible to learn to practice CBT by yourself as long as you take the required steps to get to the point where you can monitor your progress on your own.

CBT can be successfully administered in a wide variety of ways, starting with setting healthy goals, refining existing coping strategies or creating new ones, finding effective relaxation techniques, or practicing self-instruction. It can also be used in group settings just as effectively as it can be used in one-on-one scenarios. It can also be either presented directly, provided for a specific length of time, or only used briefly to help deal with a single issue. In fact, once you get to know some of the more common CBT techniques you will learn that many other self-help books are really just practicing some version of CBT. Therapists who tend to focus on this type of therapy often also expose their clients to positive stimuli as a way of creating new patterns; alternately, they may place the focus more on considering how to change the current thought process.

Common treatment

CBT is frequently used in situations where adults are aware of problems in their lives and have run out of more traditional alternatives. In scenarios like this, it has been known to successfully treat depression, anxiety, psychosis, phobias and schizophrenia. It is also effective at treating certain types of spinal cord injuries, fibromyalgia, and even lower back pain. Currently, it is also one of the most commonly used treatments for schizophrenia as well. In those who are under the age of 18, CBT is known to be an effective means of treatment for suicidal thoughts, compulsive disorders, body dysmorphia, stress disorders, and repetitive disorders. Currently, there are also ongoing studies looking into its efficacy when it comes to treating attention deficit hyperactivity disorder in people of all ages.

Anxiety: A common CBT treatment for anxiety is what is known as in vivo exposure. This type of treatment puts the patient directly into confrontation with whatever it is that causes their anxiety, whether it be a fear of being around other people or a fear of heights. The idea here is that by exposing a person to the things that cause them anxiety in the first place, it will help their minds to overwrite the maladaptive coping techniques they have been using up to this point, in real-time as they will need to come up with a new way to handle what is going on right here, right now. This process is often broken down into two parts. The first part, extinction, takes place when the old thought patterns starts to be held in less regard by the mind as it has proven to be less than useful. Next, the process of habituation begins, and a new, move effective, alternative will take its place.

Psychosis, mood disorders, and schizophrenia: The theory of cognitive depression posits that people tend to become depressed when a majority of their thought processes take on a negative bias. In individuals who are prone to depression, negative schemas start to develop early in life and are then reinforced on a regular basis.

This, in turn, leads negative biases to form based on existing negative biases that then ultimately tint the other person's entire worldview. Other common biases in those with depression include magnification, minimalization, abstraction, over-generalization, and random inference. Each of these biases can make it easier for those who are depressed to make personal inferences about themselves and the world around them that are based almost entirely on these negative, and self-perpetuating schemas.

When it comes to dealing with psychoses, CBT can be especially effective when it is paired with medication because it can be easily adapted based on the issues that each person is dealing with. It has proven especially helpful when it comes to both minimizing the chance of a relapse and also managing any relapses that do occur as effectively as possible. CBT exercises can prove to be especially effective when it comes to helping those laboring under them to question their delusions or hallucinations and help them test reality to successfully ground themselves in an undeniably true time and place. It is so effective that it is recommended by the American Psychiatric Association for these types of situations.

Deciding if CBT is right for you

While each of the exercises discussed in the following chapters are going to be more effective for treating some issues than others, this doesn't necessarily mean you are going to find something to deal with your specifics issues here. In order to determine if CBT is a good fit for you, there are some questions you can ask yourself:

- Do you prefer focusing on your current problems as opposed to those from the past?

- Do you believe that talking about your current troubles is more useful than discussing childhood experiences?

- Do you consider yourself to be primarily focused on achieving your goals in as short of a period as possible?

- Do you prefer therapy sessions where the therapist is active instead of just a passive recipient?

- Do you prefer structured therapy sessions over those that are open ended?

- Do you feel willing to put in effort on your own to support your therapy?

If you answered yes to a majority of these questions, then CBT is likely going to be effective when it comes to helping you reach your goals. While the exercises discussed in the following chapters can certainly help you deal with your issues, it is recommended that you only attempt them by yourself after you have successfully completed a guided CBT session. While there are some exercises you will be able to successfully complete by yourself, you will find that you are far more successful with the help of a professional as opposed to going it alone. Additionally, if you are dealing with any issues that may be life-threatening, it is recommended that you seek professional help as soon as possible to ensure you don't become a danger to yourself and others.

Getting the most out of CBT

If you like the idea of CBT and plan on trying it out for yourself, there are plenty of things you can do in order to ensure that you get started on the right foot. Preparing properly will not only help make the undertaking easier to manage, it will also make CBT more effective from start to finish as well.

Know what you are in for: While there are some things you won't be able to learn about your future CBT therapist until you are in the room with them, there is still plenty of research you can do early on in order to ensure they are at least going to be a relatively reasonable fit. This means you are going to want to seek out online reviews of the practitioner and also consider the types of cases that the therapist seems to take on most frequently. If you are looking for a couple's therapist, for example, a therapist who seems to work primarily with children is most likely not going to be the best choice. When in doubt, ask around; you will be surprised just how many of your friends and coworkers are seeking some type of treatment.

Prepare for change: Depending on the issues that you are dealing with, you and change might not get along terribly well right now. This is going to need to change, however, and the change will be unavoidable. CBT is about little more than change of one type or another, and you can rest assured that you will be pulled completely from your comfort zone before things are said and done. This is why you are going to need to make a promise to yourself that once you start your CBT sessions you will commit to them until they are finished. This is the only way you are going to see any effect from the process, as it requires you to commit to the process for a long enough period that new habits replace the old, negative, ones.

A big part of this means that if you find that CBT is not working for you right out of the gate, the best thing to do is going to be to try and approach it with a different attitude before abandoning it completely. If you have been tentatively open to CBT so far, for example, then you might find better success if you fully commit to the process for the remainder of your time in the program. In fact, studies show that simply making a commitment to the change that comes along with CBT at the start can make the entire process more than 30 percent more likely to prove effective in the long-term.

This is not, of course, to say that you should remain in CBT therapy forever; after all if you can't commit to the creation of new, positive habits, there isn't much that can be done for you. What's more, setting a firm end date at the start of your CBT sessions can actually make it easier to make difficult changes that you may otherwise find yourself putting off forever. It is important to consider the context that surrounds your plan for change before determining the timetable that might be reasonable to plan for your success.

Be realistic: While CBT can be extremely effective when it comes to improving specific aspects of your life, this can only be done if you take a hard look at your life and are realistic about the problems you are currently facing. This is not the time to sugarcoat things; look at your life with a critical eye, and determine just what it is you are up against. While this process will likely be difficult, it is the only way you can ever truly expect to see real improvement.

Chapter 3 How Emotions and Behavior Work

When we are young the daily decisions that we made were mainly about what we eat and what we wear were determined by someone else such as a parent or guardian. Eventually, those decisions become our own to decide. At first the decisions we make are based upon those early choices that were made for us. As our experiences move away from childhood, into young adulthood, and then on to maturity, the information and knowledge we gain broadens to include the new situations we encounter. The same can be said about how we think about ourselves, how we view the world, and how we view our future.

Developing the Ability to Think for Ourselves and Make Decisions

As we progress, we are taught how to eat, to dress ourselves, and to take care of our physical needs, and so on. How well we learn the skills we use on a regular basis can determine how smoothly our daily lives move forward. An infant does not have the knowledge to choose what type of dress might be appropriate for the current weather conditions. A toddler might be able to make a determination based upon specific clothing choices she is presented with by her mother. The mother might hold up two or three dresses and allow the little girl to choose one. Then the choice may broaden to a wardrobe of appropriate choices and a young girl will be able to mix and match them how she would like. The choices she was presented with before may have taught her that she likes the color combination of pink and purple, but she does not like brown. So what she chooses now will be based upon her personal choice and what is available in her wardrobe, but may still be guided by what her mother deems as appropriate. Perhaps her favorite pink blouse is soiled, but she wants to wear it anyway and she retrieves it from the dirty clothes hamper and puts it on herself. When she presents herself to her mother, her mother might explain that wearing dirty garments is not appropriate, especially to school or in public, and her mother may instruct her to go and change before they leave the house. Her mother may even give her a suggestion on what she feels is appropriate for where they are going.

In due course, broader experience will influence the choices in the dress that a young girl makes. Her scope of knowledge increases as well as her ability to provide herself with clothing that reflects her developing personal tastes. As she attends school, she sees the outfit another girl is wearing and decides that she likes the look and wants to wear something similar. If she has no money of her own, she may ask her mother to buy her the item. If she is successful in persuading her mother to purchase the clothing article, she adds it to her wardrobe and her choice now reflects more of her personal taste. On the other hand, suppose the mother thinks that particular style is not something she can agree to see her daughter wear and she refuses to buy it for her. The daughter can readily agree with the mother's decision or she might in a bid to establish more independence from the mother's guidelines, determine, and once she is able to, she will buy her own clothes and wear whatever she likes. As the girl matures into adulthood and has her own source of spendable income, the choices she makes about fashion and her wardrobe become her own. She may allow herself to continue making choices as to dress and grooming that are influenced by the way her mother taught her or she can decide that those previous choices do not suit the person she is becoming and learn a completely different style. Her attitude as a teenager and young adult, the stage in lifespan development when we become increasingly cognizant of who we are and the place we hold in the world, can determine the paths she will stride into her future.

Someone who is dealing with a mental illness needs simple ways to help them every day. Here are seven simple things that can help someone to think more positively and turn their day around.

1. Begin each day with an affirmation that is positive

The way a person begins their morning sets the whole mood for your entire day. We've all experienced mornings in which we woke up late which caused us to panic making the entire day feel like it was just off and disastrous. You're whole day felt negative and off because the day started with a panicked emotion that stayed with you for the entire rest of your day which bled into every other experience you had. Instead of allowing that negative feeling to remain with you all day, begin your day by having a positive affirmation. Look at yourself in the mirror and say to yourself regardless of the awkward or silly feelings "Today is and will be a good day" or something like "I'm going to be really productive and awesome today". Just by saying that to yourself will show a difference in how your day is affected.

2. Keep on the good things happening around you and to you no matter big or small

No matter what, all people encounter challenges at some point of their day and it's impossible to avoid them, days cannot statistically be perfect. At the points we are faced with those challenging moments, it's vital to keep your focus on the positive and beneficial things that have occurred. For instance, if you are running late and stuck on the subway, think about how that is a good time to finish listening to your audiobook or maybe even your favorite podcast. If a restaurant doesn't have any more of your favorite dish, take that as an opportunity which is exciting to try something new to eat.

3. During a bad situation find the humor in it

While in any situation there's always an opportunity or good time to squeeze in a good laugh to lighten the mood, even in the deepest darkest and or most trying times. Repeat to yourself that in the future this experience will be a good story to tell one day and make a good joke about what's happening. For example, you could receive the news that you'll be laid off for an indefinite amount of time. You can think of absurd ways to spend your last day or two and can think of a crazy new job that is completely ridiculous to try and find such as ice sculptor of deceased celebrities or used gum collector for the wall in Seattle.

4. Look at your failures as valuable lessons you've received

No person is perfect so it's not even worth striving for all of the time, we are all bound to make a mistake at some point or another. A lesson that we all face during our lifetime is that of failure in several different contexts including with our careers and relationships. Even though it is heartbreaking, it's good to focus on exactly how you came to that failure and analyzed exactly what you can do next time to improve your skills and avoid doing that again. Turn that failure into a lesson that allows you to be conscientious of that shortcoming that happened before to become better. Intellectualize this in solid guidelines. For instance, you made booklets that didn't have the most up to date statistics for your boss' presentation which really impacted their credibility. For future presentations, you could create a list of things you need to check will making those booklets to avoid any hiccups in the future and also increase your reliability.

5. Turn self-talk that is negative into positive self-assurance

When we are speaking to ourselves it's easy for us to be negative and often don't realize we are doing it. Many of us have thoughts like "I'm really bad with this or I probably shouldn't have even bothered trying this out". These thoughts are not healthy and don't result in anything except low self-esteem. Those thoughts eventually are internalized into negative feelings and will make those perceptions of yourself solid and very hard to erase. It's good to pay attention to your thoughts and catch yourself when you are thinking something negative and stop it from conceptualizing. Turn that negative thought into a positive one that helps you feel more self-assured. A good example of this is that "I'm really bad at speaking in front of a group of people to hey this won't be so bad I work with all these people and the more monthly meetings we have the better I'll be at it" or another example would be "I shouldn't have even tried to do this to, this didn't go as anticipated so hopefully it'll improve next time".

6. Keep your focus on the here and now and not on other points of time

By this it means the now, to be here in the present moment, not in future hours of later today or next week, but right now where you are in this precise moment. It's possible that you are getting a lecture from your boss, but in that precise moment is that the worst thing that is going on? Let go and release that comment they made a few moments ago about something irrelevant to you and let go of the possible statements he may want to say to you in a few minutes from this precise moment. Keep your attention on the current things he is saying to you now and don't concern yourself with this in the past or future. In a majority of situations, the present is not nearly as negative or intolerable as you had anticipated it to be. A large number of negative thoughts and perceptions have a stem from a memory that you have or a recent occurrence which was exaggerated for those future situations. It's important to just stay in the now.

7. Find a positive support group of friends and mentors

We are heavily influenced by the people that we surround ourselves with and when those people have positive outlooks, you'll be able to hear their positive stories and affirmations that can help you understand different ways to help you also be more positive in your life. Hearing their positive words and speech will stick with you and have a heavy influence on your personal thoughts which will in turn have influences on your words and actions which can be beneficial to the group as well. Surrounding yourself with individuals who are positive can give your life wonderful influences, however it can be challenging finding people like that. It's important to let go of and take out people that have negative impacts over your life because it feeds into your mindset and adheres to your mental illness. Do everything you can to have a beneficial and positive affect on others and that energy is contagious. Allow their positivity to influence your life in similar ways that help you work through your challenges in healthy ways.

Nearly anyone in any type of situation or experience has the ability to utilize these types of influences and lessons towards their whole lives and really increase the positivity of their attitudes. Being positive gives your life and your thoughts make positive returns, so like with anything in our lives, the more we do something and practice it, the more it will become easier and benefit our lives and others around us.

When it comes to improving our lives and having an intelligent positive outlook on things, it's beneficial to do a few things before we form our own opinions and have a particular attitude towards it. Understanding why behave, think and feel we should do the following to have well-rounded healthy conclusions:

1) Cultivate a sturdy sense of self. To know anything for sure, it's most important to first know exactly who you are as a person. By that you need to understand and know exactly what you desire out of this life and what type of thing are best for you to grow as a person. It's very important to not allow other people and outside influences dictate your opinion and perception on exactly who you should be. Marketing companies and the media tell people how they should feel, act and look, but the only person who knows that information is you. You have to do the most beneficial things for you and allow yourself to have your own preference, tastes and style.

2) Make sure you are well-informed. There are so many areas and topics out there which all people have various opinions on. Before you form an opinion, make sure you research it and know all the information there is to know about that topic or area of concern before you say in concrete facts. Building your mental resources allows you to be not only more intelligent, but very well informed by gathering, looking reading and

listening to things for yourself, rather than just taking someone's word as the concrete fact. It's important to reflect and assess the information you've discovered.

3) Be open to all options. When trying to find a good solution to a problem, being flexible is highly regarded and beneficial by looking at more than one outcome as well as looking at numerous perspectives on the subject. Look at and analyze the potential cons and pros to that situation or decision, are there positive possibilities or definite ones? Will it hurt or help anyone? What could be the consequences and are those consequences worth doing?

4) Identify probable preconceptions. It's important to analyze the influences on you and your decisions such as your culture, the way you were raised and other people's opinions. You need to look at is are you being open and fair to all parties involved? Many individuals often end up making poor decisions due to biases and the wrong ground from the beginning. When we allow ourselves the opportunity to take some time and look at information, we can make our judgements based on the observable facts we personally have seen as opposed to what other people have tried to sway us to believe. By eliminating outside influences and preconceptions we are able to make more practical and appropriate conclusions about situations.

5) Do not fasten under compression, guilt and fear. It's important to have the bravery to be able to stand up and

speak for things that you really and truly believe in and have presumed about yourself. When we just follow what the crowd is doing or saying just to avoid any confrontations and keeping the peace, we are not serving anyone in particular ourselves. It's possible you have an outstanding idea or it's the appropriate and best thing to be doing, it's important to speak up. When no other person hears your idea, healthy conversations aren't able to occur and all other potential possibilities won't happen because no one is speaking up or aware of them. Sharing your ideas not only is beneficial for the group, but also for you and your sense of self.

Chapter 4 Emotional Intelligence and Delaying Gratification

I am guessing you do know about the famous 'marshmallow test' of emotional intelligence. If you don't, here it is:

During the 1960s, social psychologist Walter Mischel headed several psychological studies on delayed rewards and gratification. He closely studied hundreds of children between the ages of 4 to 5 years to reveal a trait that is known to be one of the most important factors that determine success in a person's life, gratification.

This experiment is famously referred to as the marshmallow test. The experiment involved introducing every child into a private chamber and placing a single marshmallow in front of them. At this stage, the researcher struck a deal with the child.

The researcher informed them that he would be gone from the chamber for a while. The child was then informed that if he or she didn't eat the marshmallow while the researcher was away, he would come back and reward them with an additional marshmallow apart from the one on the table. However, if they did eat the marshmallow placed on the table in front of them, they wouldn't be rewarded with another.

It was clear. One marshmallow immediately or two marshmallows later.

The researcher walked out of the chamber and re-entered after 15 minutes.

Predictably, some children leaped on the marshmallow in front of them and ate it as soon as the researcher walked out of the room. However, others tried hard to restrain themselves by diverting their attention. They bounced, jumped around, and scooted on the chairs to distract themselves in a bid to stop themselves from eating the marshmallow. However, many of these children failed to resist the temptation and eventually gave in.

Only a handful of children managed to hold until the very end without eating the marshmallow.

The study was published in 1972 and became globally popular as 'The Marshmallow Experiment.' However, it doesn't end here. The real twist in the tale is what followed several years later.

Researchers undertook a follow-up study to track the life and progress of each child who was a part of the initial experiment. They studied several areas of the person's life and were surprised by what they discovered. The children who delayed gratification for higher rewards or waited until the end to earn two marshmallows instead of one had higher school grades, lower instances of substance abuse, lower chances of obesity, and better stress coping abilities.

The research was known as a ground-breaking study on gratification because researchers followed up on the children 40 years after the initial experiment was conducted, and it was sufficiently evident that the group of children who delayed gratification patiently for higher rewards succeeded in all areas they were measured on.

This experiment proved beyond doubt that delaying gratification is one of the most crucial skills for success in life.

Success and delaying gratification

Success usually boils down to picking between the discomfort of discipline over the pleasure or comfort of distraction. This is exactly what delaying gratification is. Would you rather go out for the new movie in town where all your friends are heading, or would you rather sit up and study for an examination to earn good grades? Would you rather party hard with your co-workers before the team gets started with an important upcoming presentation? Or would you sit late and work on fine tuning the presentation?

Our ability to delay gratification is also a huge factor when it comes to decision making and is considered an important aspect of emotional intelligence. Each day, we make several choices and decisions. While some are trivial and have little influence on our future (what color shoes should I buy? Or which way should I take to work?), others have a huge bearing on our success and future.

As human beings, we are wired to make decisions or choices that offer an instant return on investment. We want quick results, actions, and rewards. The mind is naturally tuned for a short-term profit. Why do you think e-commerce giants are making a killing by charging an additional fee for same day and next day delivery? Today is better than tomorrow!

Think about how different our life would be if we thought about the impact of our decisions about three to five years from now? If we can bring about this mental shift where we can delay gratification by keeping our eyes firmly fixated on the bigger picture several years from now, our lives can be very different.

Another factor that is important in gratification delay is the environment. For example, if children who were able to resist temptation were not given a second marshmallow or reward for delaying gratification, they are less likely to view delaying gratification as a positive habit.

If parents do not keep their commitment to reward a child for delaying gratification, the child won't value the trait. Delaying gratification can be picked up only in an environment of commitment and trust, where a second marshmallow is given when deserved.

Examples of gratification delay

Let us say you want to buy your dream car that you see in the showroom on your way to work every day. You imagine how wonderful it would be to own and drive that car. The car costs $25,000, and you barely have $5000 dollars in your current savings. How do you buy the car then? Simple, you start saving.

This is how you will combine strong willpower with delayed gratification.

There are countless opportunities for you to blow money every day such as hitting the bar with friends for a drink on weekends, co-workers visiting the nearest coffee shop to grab a latte, or buying expensive gadgets. Every time you remove your wallet to pay, you have two clear choices: either blow your money on monetary pleasure or wait for the long-term reward. If you can resist these temptations and curtail your expenses, you'll be closer to purchasing your dream car. Making this decision will help you buy a highly desirable thing in future.

Will you spend now for immediate gratifications and pleasures, or will you save to buy something more valuable in the future?

Here is another interesting example to elucidate the concept of delayed gratification. Let us say you want to be the best film director the world has ever seen. You want to master the craft and pick up all skills related to movie making and the entertainment business. You visualize yourself as making spectacular movies that inspire and entertain people for decades.

How do you plan to work towards a large goal, or the big picture (well, literally)? You'll start by doing mundane, boring, uninspiring jobs on the sets such as being someone's assistant, fetching them a cup of coffee, cleaning the sets, and other similar boring chores. It isn't exciting or fun, but you go through it each day because you have your eyes firmly fixated on the larger goal, or bigger picture.

You know you want to become a huge filmmaker one day and are prepared to delay gratification for fulfilling that goal. The discomfort of your current life is smaller in comparison to the pleasure of the higher goal. This is delayed gratification. Despite the discomfort, you regulate your actions and behavior for meeting a bigger goal in the future. It may be tough and boring currently, but you know that doing these arduous tasks will give you that shot to make it big someday.

Delayed gratification can be applicable in all aspects of life from health to relationships. Almost every decision we make involves a decision between opting for short-term pleasures now and enjoying bigger rewards later. A burger can give you immediate pleasure today, whereas an apple may not give you instant pleasure but will benefit your body in the long run.

Stop drop technique

Each time you identify an overpowering or stressful emotion that is compelling you to seek immediate pleasure, describe your feelings by writing them down. Make sure you state them clearly to acknowledge their existence.

Have you seen the old VCR models? They had a big pause button prominently placed in the middle. You are now going to push the pause button on your thoughts.

Focus all attention on the heart as it is the center of all your feelings.

Think of something remarkably beautiful that you experienced. It can be a spectacular sunset you witnessed on one of your trips, a beautiful flower you saw in a garden today, or a cute pet kitten you spotted in the neighborhood. Basically, anything that evokes feelings of joy, happiness, and positivity in you. The idea is to bring about a shift in your feelings.

Experience the feeling for some time and allow it to linger. Imagine the feelings you experience in and around your heart. If it is still challenging, take deep breaths. Hold the positive feeling and enjoy it.

Now, click on the mental pause button and revisit the compelling idea that was causing stressful feelings. How does it feel right now?

Now write down how you are feeling and what comes to mind. Act on the fresh insight if it is suitable.

This process doesn't take much time (again, you are craving instant gratification) and makes it easier for you to resist giving in to temptation. The real trick is to change the physical feeling with the heart to bring about a shift in thoughts and eventually, actions. You don't suffocate or undermine your emotions.

Rather, you acknowledge them and then gently change them. When your emotions are slowly changing, the brain tows its line which makes us think in a way that lets us act according to our values and not on impulse or uncontrollable emotions.

Self-mastery is the master key

According to Walter Mischel, "Goal-directed and self-imposed gratification delay is fundamental to the process of emotional self-regulation." Emotional management, or regulation and the ability to control one's impulses, are vital to the concept of emotional intelligence.

Mischel's research established that while some people are born with a greater control for impulses, or better emotional management, others are not. A majority of people are somewhere in between. However, the good news is that emotional management, unlike intelligence, can be learned through practice. EQ isn't as genetically determined as cognitive abilities.

Impulse control and delayed gratification

Have you ever said something in anger and then regretted it immediately? Have you ever acted on an impulse or in haste only to regret it soon after the act? I can't even count the number of people who have lost their jobs, ruined their relationships, nixed their business negotiations, and blown away friendships because of that one moment when they acted on impulse. When you don't allow thoughts to take over and control your words or actions, you demonstrate low emotional intelligence.

Thus, the concept of emotional intelligence is closely connected with delaying gratification. We've all acted at some point or another without worrying about the consequences of our actions. Impulse control, or the ability to construct our thoughts and actions prior to speaking or acting, is a huge part of emotional control. You can manage your emotions more efficiently when you learn to override impulses, which is why impulse control is a huge part of emotional intelligence.

Ever wondered about the reason behind counting to ten, 100, or 1000 before reacting each time you are angry? We've all had our parents and educators counsel us about how anger can be restrained by counting up to ten or 100. It is simple, while you are in the process of counting, your emotional level is slowly decreasing. Once you are done with counting, the overpowering impulse to react to the emotion has passed. This allows you act in a more rational and thoughtful manner.

Emotional intelligence is about identifying these impulsive reactions and regulating them in a more positive and constructive manner. Rather than reacting mindlessly to a situation, you need to stop and think before responding. You choose to respond carefully instead of reacting impulsively to accomplish a more positive outcome or thwart a potentially uncomfortable situation.

Here are some useful tips for delaying gratification and boosting your ability to regulate emotions:

- Have a clear vision for your future

Delaying gratification and controlling impulses or emotions becomes easier when you have a clear picture of the future. When you know what you want to accomplish five, eight, ten, or 15 years from now, it will be a lot easier to keep the bigger picture in mind if you come across temptations that can ruin your goal. Your 'why' (compelling reason for accomplishing a goal) will keep you sustained throughout the process of meeting the goal. Have a plan to fulfill your goal once you have a clear goal in mind. Identifying your goals and planning how you'll get there will help you resist the temptation more effectively.

- Find ways to distract yourself from temptations and eliminate triggers

For instance, if you are planning to quit drinking, take a different route back home from work if there are several bars along the way. Instead of focusing on what you can't do, concentrate on the activities you are passionate about. Surround yourself with positive people and activities that will help you dwell on your goal. Avoid trying to fill your time with material goods.

- Make spending money difficult

If you are a slave to plastic money and online transactions, you are making the process of spending money too easy for your own good. Paying with cold, hard cash can make you think several times before spending. You'll reconsider your purchases when you pay with real money rather than plastic. Take a part of your salary and put it into a separate account that you won't touch. Make sure that accessing your savings account won't be easy.

• Avoid 'all or nothing' thinking

Most of us think resisting temptation or giving up a bad habit is an 'all or nothing challenge.' It is natural for a majority of normal human beings to have a minor slip here and there. However, that doesn't mean you should just fall off and quit. Occasional slip-ups shouldn't be used as an excuse to get off the track. Despite a small detour, you can get back on the track. Don't try to convince yourself to wander in the opposite direction.

• Make a list of common rationalizations

Find a counterpoint or counterargument for each. For example, you were angry for just five minutes, or you are spending only ten dollars extra. Tell yourself that five minutes of anger is 150 minutes a month wasted in anger or ten dollars extra is $3,000 extra spent throughout the year.

Chapter 5 The Basic Premise of CBT and How it Can Benefit You in Daily Life

Cognitive-behavioral therapy was developed during the 1960s by the hypothesis that more than a situation itself, it is how we view a situation that affects our feelings. For instance, if two people get into an argument, they may each experience vastly different feelings, even though they were both a part of the same situation. One individual may view the situation as a worst-case scenario, worrying that they have lost a friend and that they will never be able to resolve the argument. By viewing the situation in this way, the first individual will feel hopeless, depressed, and anxious.

On the other hand, while the second individual is also upset about the argument, they feel much more balanced emotions. Instead of feeling hopeless they feel hopeful that the situation can be remedied. Instead of feeling depressed and anxious, they feel stressed, but still have hope that their friendship will ensure, helping to keep the second individual calm. The second individual can feel calm and hopeful in spite of the stress of the argument because of how they view the situation. Unlike the first person, they don't view the situation as a worst-case scenario; instead they view it as a normal part of friendship and interaction. By keeping in mind that conflict is normal and can be dealt with, the second individual is better able to cope emotionally, thus allowing them to also handle the situation better.

These two individuals illustrate how during daily life the way we view our circumstances shapes our emotions. If you spill a glass of milk, you can view the situation in multiple ways. You can either view it as another failure in your life or you can view it as a simple slip up that's easily remedied. The way we view our everyday circumstances shapes our emotions and feelings, which then create habits that we continue to follow in the future. This is the most basic premise of cognitive-behavioral therapy or CBT.

How we view a situation, which leads to the development of our feelings, is known as the cognitive model. This model explains how our views are formed. By understanding this model, we can begin to change our views for the better, thereby positively affecting our worldview, emotions, and reactions. This cognitive model has three parts which are:

1. Core belief
2. Dysfunctional assumptions
3. Negative automatic thoughts

From these three aspects of the cognitive model, the core belief is what you begin with, which then leads to the development of dysfunctional assumptions and negative automatic thoughts, in turn. What are these core beliefs? Put simply, they are the beliefs we hold onto deeply without even realizing it. These beliefs were formed during our childhood, early life, and lived experiences and make up what we believe about the world, others, ourselves, and even the future. We unconsciously hold these thoughts to be absolute truth, unwavering in our belief.

Example of core beliefs includes believing "I'm worthless" about yourself, "the world is cruel" about the overall world and others, and "nothing good will come" about the future.

Our rigid and extreme beliefs are known as dysfunctional assumptions. These assumptions do not truly reflect reality; they are excessive and over-generalized. The problem with these assumptions is that they frequently get in the way of our goals and emotional well-being instead of promoting positive outcomes. Common themes for dysfunctional assumptions are categorized as being based on control, achievements, and acceptance. Some examples include thinking "If I can't do it perfectly, then I might as well not do it at all." "If they dislike me then something must be wrong with me." and "It's a sign of weakness to ask for help."

Negative automatic thoughts are the third and final phase of the cognitive model. While our core belief is usually subconscious - and we are usually unaware of our dysfunctional assumptions - negative automatic thoughts take place in our conscious mind. We are aware of these thoughts, even if we don't realize the harm that they are causing us. These thoughts are involuntary and are most negative in people with depression, anxiety, post-traumatic stress disorder, and obsessive-compulsive disorder. People with these disorders often think of a situation as more disastrous or harmful than is true and also underestimate their ability to cope with the situation. Thoughts such as "I'm completely useless" "I made a mistake, now everything is ruined" "If I try I'll only fail, so what's the point" "If I don't get this job I'll never get one" and "Bad things always happen to me" are all examples of negative automatic thoughts.

With cognitive behavioral therapy, the cognitive model of these three processes is used in order to understand a person's thoughts behind their emotions. If you can alter the initial thoughts and replace them with something better and more truthful, you can, in turn, change your feelings. For instance, if a person is feeling overwhelmed it might be because their core belief is "If I can't do something perfectly then I might as well not try at all" and their negative automatic thought could be "I made a big mistake that can't be fixed" - leading them to want to quit. In order to fix the feeling of being overwhelmed, the person can then deal with the actual problem, adjusting their thoughts to something more accurate and positive. This is much more effective in changing feelings than covering up your feelings with insincere platitudes.

There are many ways in which to address these core beliefs, dysfunctional assumptions, and negative automatic thoughts. With cognitive behavioral therapy, there are formulas that are used to treat various core beliefs. Various types of core beliefs are sorted into categories, and then formulas are created for each category. This enables a person to narrow down what category their individual core beliefs fit into, allowing them to then know which formula of CBT is best suited for therapy.

With cognitive behavioral therapy, a person is taught how to help themselves independently. Yes, many people are guided through the process of CBT by their therapist. Although, the basic principles of this therapy teach the individual how to help themselves, even without a therapist. This is great, as a person can get the help they need even if they are unable to see a professional for one reason or another. You can learn the knowledge and tools you need to correct your maladaptive thought and behavior patterns, creating room for something much healthier. If you are diligent and take small steps daily to correct your cognition, you can create a healthier and happier you.

When a therapist is using cognitive behavioral therapy with their patient, the two work together, hand-in-hand. The therapist will help their patient discover which of their cognitions and behaviors are maladaptive or harmful. Once they isolate specific cognitions, these will then be analyzed, tested for their validity, and then if they are deemed to be untrue or harmful - the therapist will help their patient make revisions. The purpose of this process is to help the patient learn how to identify and manage problems, allowing them to gain the skills to do this on their own so that the training wheels can come off, allowing the individual to excel independently.

Rather than focusing on the past or the future, as some forms of therapy do, cognitive-behavioral focuses on the here and now. Instead of taking a wandering path around your problems to find a solution, you can directly confront your problems and fix them to see real and solid results. If you are struggling to heal after a traumatic event or struggling with daily anxiety when faced with interacting with other people, you don't have to talk about your childhood or your dreams to fix your problems. The approach CBT takes is much more straight-forward. By knowing what is causing you problems your distorted cognition can be revealed, and once this distortion is made plain to see it can be changed for the better.

Often, when working on improving a problem, you will set goals for yourself to track improvement and help yourself know what might or might not be working. These goals should fit the SMART standard of being specific, measurable, achievable, relevant, and timely. Not all of these goals have to be big - most of them will be small baby steps - but having something specific to work toward will motivate and encourage you. These goals will be different for every person depending on their common obstacles and troubles. For instance, a person with a social anxiety disorder may have the goal to be able to talk to strangers, be more assertive, or perform on stage. Likewise, a person with the major depressive disorder might have the goals of reaching out to friends, getting out of the house, and opening up about their feelings. No matter your reason for choosing cognitive behavioral therapy, a core principle is setting SMART goals to help you move forward and make actionable and effective change. For this goal setting, a person will have to analyze themselves and decide what goals are important to them, what goals will help them recover. These goals aren't always easy, sometimes they are frightening, but you can start small and work your way up to the more difficult ones. Once you obtain your baby step goals, you can then create a new list of steps that make it a little further and further until you have obtained your overarching goal of a better life.

Cognitive-behavioral therapy is named thus as its purpose is to change how a person thinks, otherwise known as their cognition, and how they act, which is their behavior. To this end, CBT uses multiple techniques that pinpoint both the cognitive and the behavioral aspects of a person to direct change and growth. The exact techniques will vary from person to person and case by case, but many of the techniques that people use share similarities. These techniques can be slightly altered for the individual as they are highly versatile. We will go into these methods and techniques into great detail later on in this book. However, for the moment, let's look at brief synopses of some of the more prominent and popular techniques so that you can develop a good understanding of what will be used later on.

Journaling:

There are a couple of types of journaling that are frequently used in CBT. While some people may keep general journals to work through their emotions and circumstances, there is a specific thought journal that is vital to the therapy process. This thought journal catalogs thoughts and feelings, their intensity, how you reacted to them, what supports the thoughts or feelings, or disproves the thoughts or feelings, whether they were proven to be true or false, and new healthier thought. For instance, if your initial thought was that everyone must hate you, this thought will then be disproved and replaced with a more balanced and healthier thought. By keeping this journal, you can begin to recognize your negative thought patterns and slowly work on confronting them and replacing them with something healthier. It will take time, but it has been proven to be effective. While a regular journal isn't always used with CBT, it remains a vital part of the process; everyone is encouraged to keep one of these thought journals.

Cognitive Restructuring:

In order to restructure our cognition, we must first start by unraveling its distortions. To do this, we must become more intimately aware of ourselves, not hiding from who we are but truly allowing ourselves to see what distortions we are suffering from. Once we isolate these distortions and what they are, we begin to analyze how and why they were formed. Now that you understand this distortion, you can begin to challenge it, beginning the process of restructuring.

For instance, if you believe that you are worthless and are struggling to love yourself or treat yourself kindly, you will need to directly confront these feelings of worthlessness. Instead of uncritically accepting this idea that you are worthless, you will take some time to consider what makes a person either lack or hold worth. Once you have considered what true worth consists of, you can then see the many areas in which you are a worthwhile human being.

Exposure and Response Prevention:

This method may be used with some anxiety disorders, but the most common and effective use for this technique is in the treatment of obsessive-compulsive disorder, or OCD. Some people think of OCD is simply being a little too tidy, enjoying cleaning, or liking office supplies. The truth is that none of these are factors of OCD. This disorder is quite literally an obsession that a person feels compelled to act on. For instance, a person may feel that if they don't flick the light switch precisely ten times after entering a room that something dreadful will happen. They might not be able to say what will happen, but the intensity of the feelings is equal to as if the entire building were to explode if they don't act on the obsession. People have many types of OCD; sometimes it includes germs, but there are many other types where germs play no role in the person's obsession.

To treat OCD with cognitive behavioral therapy exposure and response, prevention is used as an effective technique. This technique should start small and gradually increase in intensity, as the person will be exposing themselves to their compulsive behaviors but will try to refrain from acting on the behaviors. This can be incredibly difficult, which is why the method should always use baby steps at a pace the person is comfortable with. Once an individual practices exposing themselves to a compulsion without responding to it, they may journal about the experience and how it made them feel. This can give them greater insight into their feelings, and it can help to reflect on in the future as they continue to work through later stages of this technique.

Play Out the Script:

This method is most frequently used for people who struggle with anxiety disorders or phobias, though it may also help people undergoing other types of stress and fear. With this technique, a person who is prone to debilitating anxiety or fear conducts a thought experiment allowing them to imagine possible worst-case scenarios. The person allows the script of the scenario to play all the way through, seeing that even if what they fear does occur, they will still be able to handle it.

This does not work with all types of fears, but there are many situations in which it is applicable. For instance, if a person is having anxiety about running late to an appointment, their test scores, or giving a speech - then this technique can help.

Progressive Muscle Relaxation:

If you are familiar with mindfulness practices, then you are likely also aware of progressive muscle relaxation. With this technique, a person focuses on relaxing one set of their muscles at a time, until all the muscles in their body are relaxed. You can either do this on your own or with audio guidance, and either sitting up in a chair or laying down, making it easy to practice whenever and wherever you need. This technique is great for helping soothe a hyperactive mind or calm nerves, making it a wonderful option for the treatment of people with anxiety disorders.

Breathing Exercises:

Along with the previous technique, this will be familiar to people who practice mindfulness or meditation. Breathing exercises are a wonderful way to relax. This technique uses controlled and timed breathing to forcefully relax the body and mind. You can practice this method either on your own or with audio to walk you through the process.

This technique can be helpful regardless of the diagnosis. It does not matter if you have depression, anxiety disorder, obsessive-compulsive disorder, or simple day-to-day stress.

Activity Scheduling:

With activity schedules, a person has scheduled pleasurable activities to enjoy, which is to help the person treat depression and anxiety by systematically increasing the number of pleasurable experiences. It may take time for a depressed person to enjoy their favorite activities again, but by increasing their frequency, the person will gradually improve. To do this, the person should have a list of pleasurable activities, and then every week they should set aside time within their schedule to complete at least one of these activities. Larger activities such as going to the movies may only occur once a week, whereas smaller activities like enjoying a favorite snack should be enjoyed daily. Over time, this process will increase the number of pleasurable experiences, establish a daily routine, and increase the person's problem-solving abilities.

Behavioral Experiments:

Often used with people struggling with anxiety disorders, behavioral experiments allow a person to overcome their catastrophic thinking and replace it with something much more realistic and balanced. For instance, if a person feels that if they start participating in a local support group, that something terrible will happen, the person will put it to the test. To do this, they will write out what their fear is, test out the hypothesis by completing the test and then evaluate it to see if their fear was true or not. This means that the person may try attending one of the meetings of the local support group, and then afterward they will assess if their fear of something terrible happening came true or not. With this technique, a person can overcome their anxiety and negativity.

There are many techniques involved in cognitive behavioral therapy. Not all of these techniques are required to be used by the same person, as the techniques needed will vary based on the person's individual condition. However, no matter which of the above techniques are needed, CBT has been proven time and again to be effective. Many studies and reviews have demonstrated this method of therapy to be constructive in the treatment of mental illnesses, such as depression or an anxiety disorder. In fact, it has been proven through multiple professional studies that a person is much less likely to experience a relapse in their depression over time if they use CBT as a therapy method.

Beginning with cognitive-behavioral therapy does not have to be difficult, you can easily learn how to adopt this amazing therapy for the better of both your present and future.

Chapter 6 Maintain Awareness

Avoiding situations that bring you harm is great. But in real life, we both know that that is not always realistic. Life throws plenty of bad situations at you and you can't avoid them all. Therefore, it is essential to develop healthy coping skills for when you do encounter these situations.

Situations that stir up mental illness symptoms can be everyday situations that other, healthier people find to be no big deal. But for you, they can feel catastrophic. They can lead you to relapse in your symptoms, after working so hard to overcome those symptoms with CBT. Learning to cope in harmful everyday situations is essential to keep yourself from falling into despair.

Anxiety

Many everyday situations that are nothing to healthy people can trigger severe anxiety in some. For instance, a huge crowd at an airport can be stressful for anyone, but it can be disastrous for you if you have agoraphobia or social anxiety. But what if you have to fly for work or to visit a sick relative? You have to be a part of that airport crowd, whether you like it or not. The situation is not ideal for you but you can use various techniques to cope with your anxiety.

The best technique is relaxation. Focus on your breathing. Breathe in through your nose, out through your mouth. By focusing on your breathing, you take your mind off of the stress that surrounds it.

Progressive muscle relaxation also is helpful in anxiety-provoking situations. First start with the muscles in your scalp. Force yourself to relax those muscles. Next move to your forehead muscles. Keep roving your mind over your body, forcing the relaxation of each of your muscle groups. The relaxation will calm you and the intense mental focus required to perform this exercise will take your mind off of your stress.

Some people find tapping to be soothing. You can repeat a mantra to yourself such as, "I will survive this. This is really not so bad" as you tap different parts of your body. The physical action of tapping paired with the repeated affirmation can help trick your mind into believing what you are saying to yourself.

Sometimes anxiety can impair your ability to focus on anything. In that case, it is essential to pick a spot on the wall and focus on it intently. Do not chase any other thoughts that enter your head. That spot on the wall is your refuge. Use it to take your mind off of the craziness raging around you and within you.

Facing Your Fears

CBT is great for helping you overcome irrational fears and phobias. This is because CBT allows you to think about your phobias and understand that they are not rational and not conducive to your peace of mind.

If you have a phobia, you may find it very helpful to write about your phobia. When it is on paper, you will begin to see how silly it really is. If you are scared of airplanes, what are the odds of a crash, really? You are far more likely to die in a car crash than a plane crash. If you are scared of dogs because of a traumatic encounter with a dog in your childhood, remember that most dogs are man's best friends and that you are a lot bigger now. Analyze your fears to see how scary they really are.

To truly overcome your phobia, you need to begin to condition yourself to it. Exposing yourself to what scares you can help teach your mind to stop fearing it as it witnesses you emerge unscathed. There are classes you can take to condition yourself to overcome fear of heights, flying, and other phobias. Consider going to the snake or spider exhibit at a local zoo to stand near the creatures that make you want to scream. You will begin to realize that your phobias do not hurt you. If you have social phobia, try taking brief walks outside and striking up a brief conversation with one stranger a day.

The above relaxation techniques can also really help you when you are feeling the vise grip of fear from a phobia. Breathe, focus, and use progressive muscle relaxation to bring yourself out of your fear.

Handling Depression

The hardest part of coping with depression is that depression cripples your will to do anything. You may not even have the energy to get out of bed, let alone perform CBT on yourself. But coping with your depression gets easier when you begin to change your thinking to more positive thoughts. Positive thinking has the ability to release feel-good hormones like serotonin in your brain, allowing you to feel better and begin to move forward with your life.

When you find yourself drowning in depression symptoms, there may be a reason that you feel so blue. Maybe life is just hard right now or you have not been taking care of your body. Try to identify the source of your depression and remove it from your life. Focus on the present and enjoying life right now. Life is too short to be spent suffering in your bed.

Anger Management

If you have trouble managing your anger, you need to step back and breathe when you start to see red. Use your CBT journal to write down why a situation made you mad enough to hit someone or have an outburst. Then, analyze the situation. Was it really what you thought, or were you doing something like assuming and negative labeling? Were you ignoring the positives of the situation, or of a person that angered you? Now, in the future, how can you handle this situation without hitting and throwing things and lashing out verbally? Is there something you can do that is more conducive to a reasonable solution?

Rarely is anger ever a solution. Uncontrolled anger can get you into a lot of trouble with loved ones and even the law. Breathe, and think of better ways to react to situations than angry outbursts.

Using CBT to Overcome addiction

Addiction is often referred to as an illness. Many people fail to understand that addiction is usually a symptom of a deeper illness. People use drugs, alcohol, and other addictive behaviors such as gambling to create instant gratification and numb themselves against life. These addictive behaviors offer addicts temporary pleasure that drowns out the deeper pain addicts are experiencing inside of themselves. Basically, addicts use their addictions to distract themselves, or numb themselves, from what is really wrong. When the pleasure wears off, addicts literally feel like they are in hell because they have no shield from their pain, and they desperately chase a new high or thrill to keep them in the numb, pleased state that lets them ignore their problems. Addicts often live in denial of their real problems, and engage in harmful behaviors to avoid feeling the emotional fallout from their life situations, past traumas, or their childhoods.

Since CBT can address inner thoughts and thus change outer behaviors, it offers a rich opportunity for addicts to overcome their addictions. Addicts can use CBT to identify the thoughts and emotions that drive them to use and replace those thoughts and emotions with healthier ones that do not drive them to seek numbness. It also helps them learn to avoid situations, also known as triggers, that lead to relapses. In addition, addicts can use CBT to find healthy alternatives to self-medicating using substances, shopping, gambling, eating, sex, or whatever vice they have chosen to escape their problems with.

Identify addictive behaviors and the thoughts behind them. If you suddenly crave a drug, what triggered you to want to use? Was it a tense situation, like an argument with your family or a rough day at work? Did you see someone or hear a song from your drug days that made your brain start thinking about drugs?

Chapter 7 CBT And Mood Disorders

Life is one huge challenge, there is no denying that. Formal education in industrialized countries begins at a young age. Along with that comes the pressures to do well in our education. Already we are a part of the social structure of life, there is very little alternative to this way of life. We can have different beliefs and values, but still, the pressure to do well is ever present. Some choose not to live the "norm," but for most of us, we do our best to achieve what is expected of us.

As an adult comes the pressure to do well in a career. Added to that can be the stresses of raising a family, owning a home, a car, and all the latest gadgets that technology provides. We must dress in a certain way, and please our peer groups. This type of social pressure all plays its part upon our personal stress load. Deadlines to meet, places to be, money to earn, bills to pay. It is little wonder that we desire electronic gadgets for entertainment, just to help us unwind.

Whilst social structure is important to us, it does us no harm to step out of the rushing torrent of social expectations, every now and then. We take ourselves on vacation, but even that has to be paid for, organized and traveled to. Being on vacation can be stressful for some. This is where we need to think outside the box.

Most adults arrive at a breaking point sometime in their lives. With the pressures of life comes a price, and that is called stress. It can rear its ugly head in many forms, such as insomnia or eating disorders. The combination of these effects on our bodies floods us with the chemicals meant to protect us from danger. This can be the start of a downward spiral to depression. Of course there are many different reasons for worry and depression, but they all lead to the same result, making us ill.

That's why it's so important to know your own body, including your inner mind; to know yourself. Only then can you recognize the signs that you need help. CBT is a way of providing self-help, which is a great start on the road to recovery. Calming your emotions with meditational exercises is only the first step to healing. Turning around your negative thoughts is a little harder, and takes some time to become successful.

When you've come through a healing session of around 8-weeks, the goal then is to stay healed. There is no point in curing your anxieties only for them to resurface a few months down the line. It is so important to make sure you always recognize when stress is knocking on your door. Nip it in the bud before the symptoms escalate.

Maintaining a Healthy Outlook

When your body perceives a threat, messages go to the brain to produce a response which results in hormonal release. That's fine when faced with danger, it helps to keep you safe as you respond fast. When the body detects danger that is not real, those hormones become toxic.

Take back control by recognizing the signs of a panic attack that is not real. Use the meditational exercises to calm your body's emergency responses. It may sound unreal, but taking charge of your thoughts helps a great deal.

Once you are calmer, the emergency response of hormones will begin to shut down. It may take a few moments as you force your body to change direction, but it can be done. Relax those muscles. Convince your inner thoughts that there is nothing to panic about. Tell yourself that the world is still turning and everything around you remains normal.

Do this over and over until those attacks come less and less. Don't allow maladaptive thoughts to fuel your emotions. When you feel your body going into panic mode, stop whatever you are doing and take action, such as:-

Close your eyes and start your breathing exercises.

Visualize pleasant thoughts to distract your mind away from the panic.

Count numbers in your head and keep counting to distract your mind into the mundane and away from the panic.

If possible, sit or lay down and then relax go through the motions of tensing and relaxing muscles in your body.

Go make a cup of tea or coffee to keep your mind distracted.

Read a book as another form of distracting your thoughts away from the panic.

It is difficult to avoid stress and anxiety completely, but what you can do is recognize it and take action.

Other factors in your life can play a part in making sure that you feel happy inside:

Spend as much time as you can with loved ones and friends.

Smile more, even at yourself in the mirror.

Take more short breaks if your day is a busy one.

Take a look at your diet and cut down on those sugars and starches as much as you can.

Take regular exercise, even if it's only walking.

Visit somewhere pleasant.

Sit on a bench and watch the world pass you by.

Go somewhere and interact with nature to recharge your batteries.

Take a good look at the world around you. Notice the little things like a bird in the sky, or an insect on the ground.

Learn to appreciate the trees and flowers. Sometimes we rush everywhere in our cars and don't have time to notice that nature is all around us.

Find time to talk to other people. After all, we are all going through the same processes. Learn to share your thoughts and others will share theirs with you. Be more tolerant of each other.

Do kind things for other people around you. It does not need to involve money. You could smile at a complete stranger. You never know they may need it. Allow someone through a door before you step through it. Give up your seat on a train. Just add your helping hand around, if only for a few moments.

Concentrate on "today." Not tomorrow or next week, only the here and now.

Expect setbacks then they won't knock you down unexpectedly. They will happen; pick yourself up, brush yourself down and move on.

Talk to yourself when no one's around. You are your best listener.

Perhaps you already practice some of our suggestions above. Learning to cope with anxious moments means re-training how you think. Once conquered, it is a new lifestyle that should stay with you for good. Think more positive thoughts and your smile will come naturally. That's because you have put stress and anxiety at bay.

Chapter 8 Mistakes to Avoid in Cognitive Behavioral Therapy

Cognitive Behavioral Therapy is a very effective method to treat a variety of psychological disorders. If you or someone you know is undergoing therapy, it helps to know what CBT is and how it is administered to a patient. Take note that not all treatments are the same. A trained therapist will know how to treat specific disorders and what kind of CBT treatments to administer to them.

While the treatment is going on, some common mistakes can be prevented to ensure that the therapy sessions go on effectively. Here are some of the common mistakes that either caregivers, patients or even doctors sometimes make, and how to correct them:

#1- Not understanding the importance of repetition for change

This is specifically for doctors. When treating patients using CBT, it is not encouraged to tell the patient how to think and immediately expect them to alter their thoughts. The element to a successful implementation of CBT was the repeating of statement that could change irrational thinking, and these statements are what the therapist must use to help these patients too.

Just because someone told them to think differently doesn't mean that they will immediately change their minds. If this were true, then nobody would need CBT because all you needed to tell someone was to think differently and they would immediately do it. With CBT, these various methods were crafted in order to provide the patient with different magnitudes to change and also for the therapist to employ different strategies to change a person's way of thinking.

A key component of CBT is repetition, and this cannot be emphasized enough and actually, it is true with any new skill that you want to change or alter or learn. A move or skill or method done thousands of times will eventually become automatic to the person. At first, things will be awkward as your body or mind has not done a certain move before. Your movements are slow as you execute a movement or you forget to think the way you are supposed to. But as you keep practicing to think or move in a certain way, each aspect of this move or thinking will become automatic the more you practice. You will be able to automatically respond or act without even thinking.

Altering the way you think is learning a new skill as well; just the same way you learn a physical skill. You can't be a good golfer if you do not practice swinging your club at least a few thousand times. According to Malcolm Gladwell in the book 'Outliers', the magic number to masterfully learn a skill, physical or mental, is by doing it for at least 10,000 hours. Successful people who are professionals in their field hone their craft or skills by spending at least 10,000 hours on it.

This does not necessarily mean that it will take 10,000 hours to change the way you think in order to have a positive impact on your life but it just gives you an idea of how much time you need to invest to make things happen or reach your goals. Frequent repetition of challenging thoughts will bring in results as you will start noticing changes in four to eight weeks of therapy. But to make it automatic, you need to consistently keep practicing.

It is the same way you have spent thousands of hours repeating irrational thoughts and most likely, your brain automatically programs to think that way.

You need to identify specific, beneficial, and positive thoughts in order for your brain to think in a different way. Keep exercising these thoughts repeatedly; especially when you feel that your mind is wandering into the negative zone.

Oftentimes, especially when you are first going through therapy, it is usually difficult to achieve this vital repetition. But this is why reading articles on CBT and understanding the mistakes that you should not be doing comes in handy. Alternatively, you can also read motivational articles or quotes and listen to audio tapes to alter your thinking.

#2- Making social comparisons and creating assumptions on CBT

Often times, when a therapist explains cognitive therapy to their patients and examine their irrational thinking and also explain why this thinking is irrational, patients usually say that it does make sense and wonder why they never thought of this before.

However, in some cases, once patients understand the process of using irrational thought challenges, they come to assume that this is the way that they should be thinking at all times, without ever examining the need to change their entire thinking process.

This will then result in the mistake of using social comparison assumptions. Most patients state "I should be able to just think this way. Everyone else doesn't have to do this (referring to the CBT methods)." This thinking is a major error as they do not realize that their assumptions about other patients not using CBT techniques are utterly inaccurate.

Anyone, whether going through irrational thinking or not, can benefit using CBT techniques, the only difference is that they may not have to go through CBT techniques related to disorders.

If you listen to how successful people or even optimistic people talk, you will recognize a pattern of how they apply positive thinking in their lives. For example, you may have heard people talk about a difficult event, but then say 'but I told myself' or 'I took a deep breath' or 'Okay, relax. Everything is going to be okay.'

What they are doing here is called self-talk to cope with the situation at hand and make sense of what's happening and react calmly before they attempt to tackle a problem.

It is wrong to assume that just because you need to mentally train yourself to learn these methods and deliberately apply them, means that you are doing something others are not doing. People all around you apply these techniques, you just either don't notice it or they do it differently from you.

The only difference here is that you learn this through therapy while other people may have been doing this naturally. There may not have role models present when you are young to learn these methods or even the opportunities to learn them while growing up. People who are successful in sports, life, in their career or relationships have all learned some methods of positive thinking therapy in their lives, and they just apply it more routinely than you do. Some people are not successful naturally.

#3- Not Making CBT Methods a Lifestyle Change

The crucial element that plenty of people do not get about CBT is that it trains the brain to react differently to situations. CBT is not about identifying the error and correcting it to bring about the impact in a patient's life. A patient may experience some benefits from altering their thoughts and lead them to believe their training or therapy is over, and they do not need to continue therapy anymore.

However, the changes we experience in cognitive-behavior needs to looked at as lifestyle change just like how you see exercise as a lifestyle change. You wouldn't sacrifice exercising for a few months, achieving your goal weight, toning your muscles, and then stopping exercising and expecting all your muscles to remain in its toned condition. It is similar to restricting calories so that you can lose weight and then not expecting to gain weight when you return to normal eating.

When you make a lifestyle change, you commit in any behavior or activity regularly in order to maintain health or good habits. Where CBT methods are concerned, the changes we make are meant to improve our emotional and mental state and well-being. We need to devote our attention to this practice in order to reap its full benefits.

The body needs constant maintenance in many ways to be in optimum health and fitness, and people have come to realize that. However, the same does not apply to the brain as plenty of people think that they don't need maintenance. While people do take CBT and obtain its initial benefits, rarely do they look at it as a lifestyle change and will most likely revert to the old ways of thinking, the patterns and behaviors, unless they take conscious efforts to ensure that they practice CBT daily or frequently.

Practicing CBT on a daily basis such as relaxation methods would be in times of stress. To reduce the stress you experience, you may use the CBT relaxation methods. Most people would think that they feel good anyway on a daily basis, so they don't need relaxation anymore. But that isn't the case. Practicing relaxation techniques even when you do not feel stressed helps to eliminate symptoms related to stress.

#4- Not Using Relaxation Regularly

Another mistake patients and caregivers make is that they believe that the benefits of relaxation are obtainable despite only practicing it infrequently. Patients or clients report being stressed and anxious to their therapist and when asked how often do they find time to meditate or do relaxation techniques, they usually either say once or not at all. These same clients, on the other hand, report positive feedback when they employ relaxation techniques.

Your mind and body will be exercised to respond to situations in a different way when you practice relaxation exercises frequently. This practice is extremely powerful.

For example, work stresses can cause your body to react with certain symptoms such as when you drive by your workplace on your days off. Our bodies have a tendency of associating a type of stress with a person, a thing or a stress. On the other hand, our bodies can also become accustomed to relaxation responses. You would be surprised how your body and mind can have a response to certain relaxation methods such as listening to particular music. This is why audio tapes for relaxation and meditation are powerful because the moment the body hears it, it has a tendency of becoming soothingly peaceful.

#5- Expecting Results without Practice

Patients also feel that just because they went through a few relaxation techniques, that is enough already. Say for example if you were playing football, would you be confident enough to properly kick the ball when you have never even tried doing that before? Surely, not! To ensure that your CBT techniques are effective, you should keep practicing them so that when you do experience an episode, your body and mind automatically knows how to deal with it.

CBT techniques are not the same as how you do your normal breathing every day. In order to know how to react and adapt to difficult situations, you need to practice CBT on a daily basis. Just because breathing is something that you do every time, every second, some people assume that they would be able to control it at will.

The error here is that yes, you have been breathing your entire life, but you have not been regulating your breathing at will. When you experience an anxiety or panic attack, there are plenty of other things happening to your body and mind at the same time, making it hard for you to focus on calming yourself and your breathing. Regulating your breathing is different from breathing on a daily basis.

It is vital to practice regularly to achieve to change our physiological responses, especially when we feel anxious or stressed. Unfortunately, its human nature to not be able to calm ourselves, especially when we are stressing out, which is why practicing CBT is key to mastering the techniques to respond calmly, especially if we naturally get stressed quickly. For some people, it's easier to stay calm but for most with certain disorders, practice is everything in CBT.

#6- Assuming that CBT is just about Positive Thinking

CBT is not all about thinking positively. We talk about positive thinking as a reactive to when situations become negative. However, positive thinking is just as problematic and irrational as negative thinking. Take for instance if something catastrophic is happening and you are positive at that time and think 'Everything is going to be ok' and because of this, you do not take the necessary steps to control or act or react in a situation, thus making it worse or even endangering your life. There are situations that would require us to be positive, but there are also situations where we need to be concerned and act fast to take the appropriate action. There will also be times that negative thinking can bring about a positive outcome.

What cognitive therapy does is not to lull clients into a false sense of security rather it enables them to approach life situations in a realistic manner. If we worry about issues that are less likely to happen, then we are getting worked up for nothing and would only make things worse or if we are too relaxed and optimistic about something when in actual fact, you need a fast response, things happen badly too.

CBT just helps clients to look at these situations practically and realistically. It is about assessing our thoughts so that we can take the most practical and reasonable approach.

#7- Thinking that emotions are irrational

The other side of the spectrum of CBT is that people think that emotions are not a good thing. One of the main founders of cognitive therapy, Albert Ellis, says that we are always rational, we would not feel anger. How is that possible when all of us as human beings feel things and are created to have emotions?

This concept is extremely misleading, not to mention a dangerous thought exercise. We human beings are emotional and these emotions make up an important aspect of our processing system that actually keeps us rational. They allow us to become aware of the issues you are facing and actually address them appropriately. No human being can be free of emotions and it is healthy to have emotions. Extreme emotions though, need to be kept in check.

Without emotions, we miss important aspects of our environment. Our initial emotional reactions prepare us to face situations, whether to fight or to flee, and this intellectual response determines what emotion helps us make the better decision. No doubt that our emotions are the one that causes us to overreact but these emotions sometimes make us more acutely aware of our surroundings. Say perhaps you are walking in a dark alley and you feel threatened when you are really aren't. We prevent a false sense of security but become more aware of the things around us.

However, if we keep overreacting to every situation, this is where CBT can help. CBT can help us understand how to identify when we may be overreacting and also to keep our emotions in perspective.

Over the years, to prevent overreacting, therapists have used CBT but have found that it was too limiting until it inhibited the processing of emotions. Thus, therapists moved towards a more mindfulness-based CBT, known as MCBT, which focuses on learning to tolerate different emotional states rather than eliminate them.

#8- Placing Demands on Rationality

Being rational is a good thing and it benefits us greatly, but that does not mean that you SHOULD be rational ALL THE TIME. Saying that you should be rationale all the time is an irrational statement in itself. First, this is a perfectionist demand and second, CBT is about decreasing stress by cultivating realistic expectations. Third, this statement is irrational because of the idea that if something is bad, the opposite is good.

CBT is about finding balance. With clients who are anxious, therapists usually employ exposures to provoke anxiety so that patients have the opportunity to train to defuse the situation. If you are worried or afraid of something, then you need to face it.

But it isn't the case all the time. It is not always good to challenge fear. Sometimes, it helps to just run away from it.

This attitude can bring unnecessary stress which could interfere with a person's progress in the fears that are much more important to face. Evaluating a fear is vital because a person can then decide on what affects their satisfaction and how to overcome or deal with it.

#9 - Not Taking Responsibility for Change

We also need to stop using CBT as an excuse to not try to change or change. CBT does teach a person to appreciate and recognize all aspects for themselves and it is meant to be used to create a foundation that provides a stable foundation that people can make changes. Those undergoing CBT understand that the therapy does make your feel good thus giving a person greater confidence to try new things and make better improvements in their life. Accept your flaws and understand that there are some areas in your life that need change and needs improvement, especially when these areas are destructive to you and the people around you. Do not feel bad about acknowledging the existence of this flaw. Accept yourself, flaws and all, but work on these flaws to become a better person.

Some people, though, take this as a justification for not taking responsibility for the changes that are taking place. They tell themselves that they are fine just the way they are or they focus entirely on a cognitive belief without any consideration of the complexity of the situation. CBT should not be used as a justification for inappropriate or unhealthy behavior. It is meant to be used to help people examine their thought processes and choices so that it can improve their life and relationship. It is not meant to continue problematic attitudes.

#10- Placing Demands on Mindfulness

Another mistake that we often make, whether as patients, as caretakers or as a therapist, is to place demands or expectations on the practice of mindfulness. The issue here is that these expectations prevent us from experiencing mindfulness in a more mindful way. Part of CBT is to understand that mindfulness is a process that will take time and patience, not thousands of years, but just a little while. Mindfulness is a process that will come to you without any expectations and it is different for different people.

The critical concept here is to not try to reach mindfulness. Instead of trying to be mindful, just allow yourself to be mindful, the more you remove the demands, the more you will achieve.

Chapter 9 Cognitive Behavioral Therapy Techniques

Despite the fact that cognitive behavioral therapy has a specific structure it aims to follow, it is actually quite flexible. There are many different techniques used during therapy that teach the coping skills necessary to see a reduction in distressing symptoms. Since this form of therapy can be used for virtually anything under the sun, from debilitating phobias to psychosis, it has to have a wide range of tools available to treat individual symptoms and situations. Each and every one of these techniques aims to help change negative or unproductive thought pattern, self-defeating attitudes, and help regulate moods.

Cognitive restructuring is the quintessential technique thought of with cognitive behavioral therapy. This is literally the act of identifying and reshaping thoughts in an effort to change thoughts and behaviors. As previously discussed, this often employs journaling, recording thought patterns, and creating plans for healthier, more productive thinking patterns. By altering the thought patterns, your feelings and therefore, behaviors, also change. For a more in-depth understanding of this technique, see Breaking Free from Negative Thoughts.

Exposure therapy is another common technique focused on exposing an individual to something they fear. As anxiety and fear go hand in hand, by treating fears, anxiety is treated as well, making this an effective treatment for those with anxiety problems. Upwards of 80% of patients experience a noticeable decrease in their anxiety with this sort of therapy. It works with the logic of we naturally seek to avoid things which cause us to feel fear, which naturally reinforces the instinct to avoid things that evoke fear. It is a sort of defense mechanism to keep yourself away from dangerous, fear-evoking stimuli in order to keep yourself alive and alert. The downside to this is that the more we avoid the things we fear, the worse the fear becomes, and the fear begins to spread to other, similar stimuli.

For example, someone may have a fear of driving over bridges, but unfortunately for her, she lives in a town in a mountain valley with a river through the middle of it and crossing bridges happens regularly. She dislikes the idea of driving with nothing between herself and the water below her except for stone suspended in midair. Eventually, she finds the act of driving over a bridge so distressing that she goes out of her way to avoid driving over the local bridges, even if that means her choices of restaurants, stores, and activities are drastically limited by avoiding half of her town. Soon, her anxiety over falling off of a bridge transforms into anxiety about falling off of a mountainside. The two are not that different, after all; both involve her free-falling if she is losing control of her car, but in one scenario, she plunges into the water, and in the other, and her car hits solid land. She begins to avoid driving on mountainside roads to avoid the feelings of anxiety, but this too is difficult as she lives in a town in a mountain valley. She eventually finds herself so used to worrying about where she is driving and whether she will crash, that she begins to avoid driving altogether because the entire act of driving has become too distressing. After a while of leaving her anxiety unchecked, she begins feeling intense anxiety even just sitting in her car.

Through exposure therapy, however, this anxiety can be lessened, and eventually, treated. This process enables you to establish brief contact with your deepest fears long enough to realize that the negative results you are expecting will not happen. In doing this, anxiety lessens, called habituation. Slowly, you build up a tolerance for whatever you feared, and over time, you stop feeling anxiety when confronting your fear. This can be done entirely at your own pace; the idea is to slowly warm up to the idea that whatever you are facing will not overwhelm you, and as such, taking the approach of tossing yourself all in and causing yourself to experience anxiety would not be the best way to accomplish this goal. You should start with the least anxiety-inducing exposure possible and work your way up as your tolerance builds. The exposure can take any form, physical, as thoughts, or watching representations of whatever the fear is. So long as it increases your tolerance for what evokes fear, it is an effective form of exposure. For the woman afraid of driving, she could start by looking at a car, then moving toward playing with a toy car, eventually driving the toy car over a bridge. Then, she would begin talking about driving a car over a bridge, followed by watching a video of a car driving over a bridge. She would work up to sitting in her car as a passenger, eventually with the car being driven on flat roads, and eventually up hills, then mountains, and along bridges. After adjusting to riding over bridges, she could begin driving her car and eventually, get to a point where she can drive over the bridge as well. This can be tailored to any fears, including thoughts or memories for people facing OCD or PTSD.

Likewise, it can be tailored into small steps to aid in motivation for those suffering from depression. Going to class might be too big of a step for Aidan to take all at once, but he can start by waking up on time for class one morning, and the next morning waking up and showering or otherwise getting ready for class. The next day could involve waking up on time, showering, getting ready, and taking a walk around campus, and eventually work up to actually attending his lectures. Each day brings him another step closer to attending class, which would eliminate some of his feelings of worthlessness and incapability he fosters as a result of not attending.

Behavioral Activation is a technique typically used for depression. It teaches you how to understand how your surrounding environment can influence your depression and aims to change behaviors that will either maintain or worsen your depression symptoms. While everyone faces events that can cause periods of sadness, we oftentimes turn to coping methods that work short-term but are detrimental as long-term solutions. For example, someone who has just gone through a messy divorce may decide to have a few too many drinks. Now, as a one-off, most people have been there; it is a trope to open a drink after a long or stressful day for a reason. However, when drinking, especially to excess, becomes the only method of coping with the feelings surrounding the divorce, there is a problem. Likewise, Aidan taking a day off for mental health to cope with his feelings of hopelessness would not be seen as a problem, but not going to class for the rest of the quarter is harmful to his grade, his GPA, and potentially his status as a student at that university, which negatively impacts his ability to enter the workforce. By never going to class, he misses out on the benefits of being a student, such as the social interaction he needs and the rewarding education, and potentially his career of choice. This can exacerbate the symptoms of depression, making the depressive episode last longer and adding extra stress and further perpetuating the cycle of spiraling deeper and deeper into depression.

Along with these techniques used during cognitive behavioral therapy, learning how to set goals conducive to keeping distorted, negative thought patterns at bay in the future is a necessary technique to master. Goals may seem like something that is easy to set without instruction, but there are poorly formed goals that will do nothing but add to your distress. It is incredibly important to avoid poorly formed goals in order to be successful at this step in rewiring your brain.

Common, but poorly formed goals include, "I want to feel satisfied with my life as a whole," "I want to be the person I used to be in college, or during some other time," and "I want to avoid feeling sad." Each of these looks innocent enough, but each also has a fatal error that makes them nearly impossible to fulfill, which serves to do nothing but frustrate the one trying to achieve them. The first goal seeks to reach an emotional state, but emotions are fickle and constantly changing. It is impossible to feel satisfied with everything all the time, which leaves plenty of opportunity for you to fail at succeeding. By failing, you then may fall back into distorted thinking, such as believing that you do not deserve to feel satisfied, or you will never feel satisfied. The second goal is effectively wishing to go back to the past. Just like how cognitive behavioral therapy is present-oriented, your goals should focus on the present or future. Yes, you may miss the person you used to be before a trauma, but it is impossible to return to the past. That trauma is a permanent part of who you are, and while it may not define you, you will always carry it with you. This goal renders you so fixated on the past, that you fail to recognize the person you are growing into. Instead of returning to the past, you should focus on healing the person you are now. The last goal looks well-formed, but to a trained eye, it is a negative one. It seeks to avoid something, which roots it in negative behavior. This can leave you so caught up in avoiding feeling sadness that you are constantly feeling anxious about feeling sad, which really just replaced one problem for another. Sadness is a feeling, and everyone will feel it sometimes. It is okay to feel sad sometimes, and getting caught up in avoiding it is not healthy.

With an understanding of what poorly-formed goals may look like, you now know what not to do. Now, it is time to focus on what a goal should look like. Your goal should always be something beneficial to you, whether to your physical health, your mental health, or it will bring you some sort of value in life. These goals are targets to improve your life, so they have to be things that you truly desire, not things that you feel obligated to want or pursue. When considering a goal, it is commonly recommended to use a SMART method: The goal should be Specific, Measurable, Achievable, Realistic, and Timed. By setting SMART goals, you will set yourself up to succeed, as you will have goals that are designed to be easier to achieve.

Your goal must be specific. This should be something that you would like to be able to accomplish that you will value. You could decide that you want to lose weight, or write a novel that you have had planned for years, or perhaps you want to write a song. You could also make this goal relevant to your mental health, such as wanting to develop a solid coping mechanism for your claustrophobia or to have fewer anxiety attacks. The key to this step is being sure it is something you will inherently value so it intrinsically motivates you to want to complete it. Someone completely uninterested in mountain climbing would likely not care enough to complete a goal of climbing their local mountain, and likewise, someone who does not suffer from arachnophobia has no reason to set a goal relating to tolerating being around spiders. When you make your goal incredibly specific, you know exactly what to expect, and exactly what result you are striving to achieve. For example, you could set a goal of, "I want to manage my anxiety," or you could set a goal of, "I want to reduce the number of anxiety attacks I feel by half."

Your goal must be measurable, meaning you have to be able to quantify it somehow. Saying, "I want to manage my anxiety," is not measurable, as there is no standard to check whether or not it has been achieved. Reducing the number of anxiety attacks in half, however, is measurable, as you have a specific, quantifiable result you are seeking to achieve. This could also look like setting a certain amount of time aside for a certain hobby or aiming to lose a specific amount of weight instead of saying you just want to lose some weight. The key here is to make sure you specify how much, or how often you are looking to do something.

Your goal must be achievable, preferably with milestone sub-goals to track your progress. By having sub-goals that you are meeting, you will feel good about yourself and your progress, making you more likely to continue meeting your goals in the future. If your goal is to lose ten pounds, you could aim to drop one pound per week until you achieve your goal, or if you wish to work on your agoraphobia, you could aim to spend a few more minutes outside of your home every day.

Your goal must be realistic for yourself. Recognize that what is realistic for your friend or your significant other may not be realistic for yourself, and keep that in mind when choosing a goal for yourself. Your best friend may be able to run a six-minute mile, but that would not be realistic for someone with an injury that prevents high-impact exercise. Keep in mind that in order to be realistic, your goal should be something enjoyable or pleasant for yourself. By setting a goal that you value, you are more likely to continue working toward it without becoming discouraged if you get off track. Make sure that it is something you can achieve during the time you are granting yourself, as setting yourself up with a goal that is next to impossible only sets yourself up for failure.

Lastly, your goal must be timed, meaning you should set a reasonable timeframe to complete it. Make sure you give yourself a realistic amount of time to complete your goal to avoid setting yourself up for failure. Most people cannot write an entire full-length novel in a week, and most people will not be able to shed twenty pounds in a month. When setting your goals, aiming for a mix of short and long-term goals can aid with motivation, as you will always have something to keep you motivated, while also regularly be achieving some of the goals you have set, helping better you as a person, and hopefully, bettering your mental health.

Aidan, understanding what a SMART goal entails, decides that he wants to get back into his hobby of writing for himself, hoping to once again get pleasure from what used to be one of his favorite hobbies before his depression symptoms took over his life and killed his motivation for everything. He decides that he wants to write a short book of 20,000 words, which he will add 600 to at least five days a week until it is finished. This goal is specific: it has an easily understandable ending point of being finished at 20,000 words. It is measurable, as he has a specific amount of writing he will complete altogether, as well as a plan of writing a specific amount daily. It is achievable; writing 600 words a few times a week is completely plausible, and he set his goal in such a way that he knows that every time he writes 600 words a day, he has accomplished a smaller goal, and likewise, when he manages to write five days in a week, he has accomplished another. It is realistic, as he frequently used to write at least that much on the regular, and it is something he is sure he can do. It is timed; he understands that it will take nearly seven weeks to complete all 20,000 words at 600 words a day. With his SMART goal established, he is ready to begin working toward his goal in the hopes of finding some small enjoyment. Just by getting motivated to write, and accomplishing each small daily goal, he is already combatting some of his symptoms of depression.

When setting a goal for yourself, keep in mind that while it should be a challenge to complete, it needs to be reasonably attainable. If you remember to keep your goals SMART and remember your own limits, you will see improvements in your mental health as you achieve them. For a better impact, try creating goals that go along with your positive affirmations. Aidan struggles with finding the motivation to do things because he fails to see how his actions matter, so he created an affirmation of, "I will put forth the effort because it allows me a chance to better my situation. Remaining complacent will keep me stuck where I am, and I deserve happiness." This is also applicable to his goal, as whenever he begins feeling like it does not matter if he writes, or that missing a day is no big deal in the long run because nobody cares, he can remind himself of his affirmation. He reminds himself that bettering himself and his situation is always worthwhile, and hopefully, manages to motivate himself into meeting his daily goal of writing.

Every technique discussed in this chapter is beneficial in different ways, and each is worthy of at the very least attempting. Remember that all of these techniques require time and patience before you may see results. None of these will create drastic, overnight differences, but they will change your life and your way of thinking and interacting with the world if you give them the time and perseverance they require. They will absolutely better your life, given the chance, and should be given the consideration they deserve. Cognitive restructuring reshapes your thought process, providing healthier ways of thinking. Exposure therapy can eliminate anxiety responses. Mindfulness can help you remain grounded and level-headed during emotional periods. Setting goals that are attainable, but worthwhile allows you to better yourself as a person and gives you something to work toward. With these techniques, paired with your knowledge of identifying cognitive distortions, breaking free from the distortions, and how to create beneficial affirmations, you are prepared to begin rewiring your mind. Good luck on your journey. Remember, you, like everyone else, are worthy of living a happy, mentally healthy life.

Chapter 10 How Does Age Affect The Symptoms And Onset Of Anxiety?

Anxiety is one of the few types of disorders that can be diagnosed at a young age. In fact, most children who have a diagnosis of anxiety have had it since they were seven years old. There are some differences in the way that the symptoms of anxiety will present themselves in children versus the way they will present in adults.

In younger children, anxiety symptoms may present in a variety of ways. Some of the most common symptoms include extreme worry and fear, changes in behavior, and shifts in mood, eating, and sleeping. Children with generalized anxiety disorder have a consistent worry that is present nearly every day. The most common things that cause concern to children are making mistakes, tests, and homework like many children. Yet in addition to these typical worries, children experiencing generalized anxiety disorder will also have worries about other things, sometimes over issues that we often do not align with childhood. They may feel intense worry over attending birthday parties, war, the weather, the future, illnesses, safety, getting hurt, playtime with friends, riding the bus to school, or even recess time. Dealing with all of these various types of concerns that occur on a daily basis can make it difficult for young students with generalized anxiety disorder to concentrate in school. They can have difficulty sleeping, eating, or even playing and having fun. Physical symptoms of anxiety that children often experience include an upset stomach, butterflies in the stomach, dry mouth, a racing heart, and clammy hands. While children are unable to recognize the symptoms as such, these are classic symptoms of a typical human fight or flight response. Unfortunately, in the case of anxiety disorders, this response is overly reactive and occurs regardless of whether a danger is present or not. While some children with generalized anxiety disorder will hold their worries inside, others will discuss them with adults, sometimes asking repetitive questions to ensure that everything is alright. Even with reassurance, it is difficult for children with generalized anxiety disorder to feel that they are safe and they often continue to worry themselves about the future. Separation anxiety is a common issue that children face. It is developmentally typical for all infants to go through a phase of separation anxiety and they do develop an intense fear of people who are not their primary caregivers. Separation anxiety disorder can be diagnosed when a child does not move past the stage of being afraid to leave a parent. This disorder can have an intense display of symptoms in which children become physically ill at the thought of leaving their parent, which may, in turn, cause an excessive number of absences from school. Children with separation anxiety disorder often miss standard childhood events such as birthday parties or play dates.

They may even have intense anxiety at being in a room of their home without a parent present. Social anxiety disorders often occur in children because they are concerned about how others will react to their words and actions. They do not want to seem different from their classmates and so they try to avoid being the focus of attention. They may not speak out in class or panic if they are called on to give an answer. Children may begin to avoid school in order to avoid their phobias of social distress. They may begin to feel illnesses or overtiredness before a school day begins. In some extreme cases of social anxiety disorders in children, they may develop selective mutism. This is the case of an extreme social phobia that is so difficult to manage that the child does not speak in public settings.

They will still communicate with their family members within the safe confines of their homes, but in public will choose to not speak. Specific phobias can also affect children. These go beyond normal childhood fears. Children with specific phobias develop a more intense, extreme, and long-lasting fear of something specific. Children will try to avoid their phobias to the best of their ability and may become terrified and unable to respond to comfort if they are confronted with their fear. Some common childhood phobias include blood, vaccinations, siders or other animals, the dark, and thunderstorms. The onset of anxiety in children can have many causes. Often it is a learned behavior that they have observed in the adults in their lives. It can also be an issue of genetics.

Some genes cause a child to have more of a chance of being prone to developing anxiety. If chemicals in the brain are not working correctly, anxiety can be a result. It is also possible that a child has gone through experiences in his or her life that has caused anxiety to develop. The loss of a family member, abuse, violence, and serious illnesses can all cause in the development of anxiety disorders in children. Trained therapists are able to diagnose children's anxiety disorders and will more likely than not utilize cognitive behavioral therapy in order to treat the symptoms that the child displays. With the specific case of working with children in cognitive behavioral therapy, it is important for the immediate family to be involved as well. Part of the changes to behavior will involve the family members as well. For example, parents will need to develop and use new responses to their child's anxieties and the questions that often correspond to the anxieties. The therapist will help the child to practice their new thought processes and behaviors while giving them praise and support. The parent can observe these supports and utilize them also. Treatment is very successful in most cases when the family is involved in the therapy sessions and the correct techniques are utilized in the home.

In adolescents and teenaged children, anxiety disorders typically have symptoms that include being excessively worried or fearful. According to several studies, more teenagers in the United States are experiencing severe anxiety disorders. More college students seek out counseling for anxiety currently than for depression, which is a statistic that has only recently begun this trend in the last ten years. The rise of suicides and suicide attempts in teenagers is also increasing at an alarming rate. Often, teenagers will feel stress, restlessness, and nervousness intensely when they develop an anxiety disorder. In the lives of most teenagers, school, extracurricular activities, and friendships rank of high importance. Anxiety can interfere with these daily activities and relationships. Symptoms often manifest as withdrawal and excessive displays of emotion. Headaches, stomach aches, muscle pain and tension, fatigue, and hyperventilation are all side effects that can stem from anxiety disorders in teenagers. Adolescence is a prime time for anxiety to take hold because, at this time, the body is changing in appearance.

Children of this age may have concerns about social acceptance, how they feel about themselves, and how they appear to others. When these feelings become overwhelming, some teens may isolate themselves, while others want to spend all of their time with friends, and still, others will experiment with risky behaviors such as the use of recreational drugs or promiscuity. Panic disorders typically are diagnosed in late adolescence, between 15 and 19 years old. Panic attacks, usually without noticeable triggers, severe anxiety, and other physical and emotional symptoms may begin to arise. The physical side effects of a panic attack may include shortness of breath, nausea, chest pains, and sweating. Some teenagers may develop specific phobias that are centered on certain situations or objects.

In order to qualify as a phobia, a fear must be intense and irrational. The fear may limit a teenager's activities, whether they have been avoiding social events or other typical activities. Adolescents most often display phobias that are focused on social situations or school performance. School avoidance may be the result of these phobias. This occurs when some teenagers show a reluctance to go to school. The adolescents may complain of anxieties as well as physical ailments. However, doctors generally are unable to find anything amiss that would require the students to miss school, even though their complaints may be chronic. In most cases of adolescent or teenage onset anxiety, it is very common for negative thoughts and feelings to create a rabbit hole that the child can continue to fall down as he or she adds more and more anxieties to his or her growing list. Sometimes medication or therapy is prescribed for teenagers with acute anxiety.

This is a risk, however, as medications sometimes carry high-risk side effects. Anxiety is a disorder that is equally prevalent among teenagers who have had a rough childhood, experiencing trauma and abuse, as among those teenagers who come from well-off families and have had seemingly easier childhoods. In the latter case, these children tend to be perfectionists and are always trying to top themselves to do better and be the best. Any teenager can be susceptible to developing anxiety no matter his or her background and the rates of teenage anxiety are ever climbing.

The biggest majority of mental health disorders are diagnosed in early adulthood including anxiety disorders. In most cases, when a young adult is diagnosed with an anxiety disorder, it is something that was present in adulthood but remained undiagnosed at the time. Anxiety disorders typically develop in adolescence. This is probably because the brain undergoes many changes at that time. However, in many cases, anxiety remains undiagnosed because the symptoms can be very similar to normal puberty changes. Therefore, many disorders are diagnosed in early adulthood instead. As with the development of anxiety disorders in children, genetics plays a large role. Young adults are going through many changes, both socially and mentally that can contribute to the diagnosis occurring at this time of life. Both biology and environment combine to create conditions in which anxiety can develop.

Many people develop anxiety well into their geriatric age. One-third of people who develop generalized anxiety disorder will be diagnosed after the age of 50 years old. However, the symptoms of late onset vary quite a bit from the symptoms in people who are younger at the time of onset. Due to this reason, anxiety can be missed or misdiagnosed in older patients. Many symptoms of anxiety can be confused for other conditions such as hyperthyroidism.

Diagnosis can be further compounded because the elderly tend to somatically describe their symptoms. Instead of complaining of psychological distress, older patients will often complain of symptoms such as pain. In the majority of cases, an older person will see their primary care or family doctor when they are complaining of these afflictions. A psychiatrist is trained to notice symptoms that may display as psychosomatic so they would be more likely to pick up on clues that would lead to a diagnosis of anxiety. A primary care physician may not be specifically looking for these issues and the patient masks the psychological symptoms as pain, so a misdiagnosis is more likely.

In addition to this, many geriatric patients have persistent medical conditions and anxiety can be a comorbid or underlying condition related to the medical diagnosis. Older people are more profoundly impacted by anxiety disorders. People over the age of 65 are much more likely to be hospitalized for their anxiety symptoms, up to three to 10 times as likely as people younger than 65. As geriatric patients experience an increase in their physical disabilities, there is a concurrent increase in their anxiety symptoms. As anxiety increases, the independence of the person decreases with an increase in the likelihood of entering a nursing home or assisted care facility developing. Patients experiencing anxiety in a nursing facility often have concerns over memory loss, fear of falling, and increasing medical illnesses.

Specifically, obsessive-compulsive disorder can affect people who are over the age of 65, but most of their obsessions and compulsions have a focus on the fear of committing sins and on hand washing. However, this age group has the lowest incidence of an initial diagnosis of obsessive-compulsive disorder. This is because most new diagnoses of obsessive-compulsive disorder in this age group occurs when the person has had the disorder for quite a long time but has remained undiagnosed. It is not common for symptoms to suddenly occur. Phobias are one type of anxiety that has a tendency to decrease with age. Instead, social anxiety disorder becomes more prevalent. In many cases, older people have anxiety about using public restrooms and eating in front of other people.

In conclusion, anxiety can affect people of any age group. The causes can stem from many factors including genetics, environment, and traumatic events. The symptoms that are displayed by a person who has an anxiety disorder can vary depending on the person, his or her age, and his or her unique set of circumstances. In the majority of cases, anxiety disorders develop during the late adolescent years but can remain undiagnosed until adulthood. In some cases, a diagnosis of another mental disorder or a physical diagnosis can create the right environment for anxiety to be present for a person.

At this point, you can skip ahead to if you wish to see how cognitive behavioral therapy can help you to overcome your anxiety.

Chapter 11 Cognitive Processing

The way to which the mind responds to an event or other stimuli is powerful and can cause a person to become "set in their ways" with their ability to do different things. Because of this, cognitive processing therapy is sometimes used to change the way that a person thinks of a certain situation, feeling or even a past event. It is an effective cognitive therapy technique, and it allows the person to overcome the problems that they had in the past. The first part of healing an anxiety or depressive disorder is to move forward from things that have happened in the past and that have been detrimental to the person.

Learning About It

To be able to successfully learn the right way to overcome the problems that a person has with anxiety or depression, they must first look at the past. They need to see what type of problems they had in the past, the way that their problems affected them and how they shaped them for the future of everything that they are going to be able to do. Since a person needs to get over their past before they can move toward their future, cognitive processing focuses on learning about the past and how it shaped that person.

When someone is dealing with their past, it can be quite painful. Therapists who use this method like to take the process slow and find out as much as they can about the past of the person to get the person talking about it and find out what triggers them in the process. This part of learning about the traumatic events or other past issues usually takes around four weeks for a therapist to get through. This is the first stage of the process, and each of the three stages is divided evenly. However long it will take the therapist, and the person who is receiving therapy to get through each of the problems is dependent on this first one and the length of time that it takes.

A therapist will likely ask their patient to come up with ideas about the past. Some people who are going through therapy might find that they actually have repressed memories of the past especially if it was traumatic. This is something that can be detrimental as well as good. While they are trying to get through these repressed memories, they may find something that is the true trigger to their depression and anxiety. It will allow them to see what it is and that they have one which is the first part of getting better and moving forward with their life.

If someone is able to figure out all of their repressed memories and all of the information that they hold, they will be able to learn as much as possible with their emotions and the problems that they have. It will allow them the chance to move on and make their lives better.

Accepting and Processing

Once a person has learned as much as possible about the events in their past and what has created this sort of anxiety or depression state, they will be able to begin the acceptance process. While finding the memories and looking at them clearly was certainly hard during the first step, this can be even harder because they need to "come to terms" with the problems that they had and make sure that they are doing things the right way for their memories.

Once they have taken the time to confront them, they will then need to make sure that they are accepting them. Are they still trying to repress these memories? Or, are they looking them in the face and acknowledging that they are there and they are making problems for the people who need to "get over" the hump of traumatic memories? Once they have learned how to, essentially, look their bad memories in the eye, they will then be able to say that they have officially accepted the memories.

One of the biggest parts of this process is not putting the blame on another person or situation that the person is in while they are repressing memories and trying to recall them. For example, someone may be tempted to think about a traumatic event and blame it on their parents, the person who was with them or even themselves. They need to let go of this blame. They will never have full acceptance of the memory and the trauma that it caused until they are ready to stop blaming someone else, something else or even themselves for the problem. Placing blame with a cognitive processing will not fix the problem or even put a name to the problem, it will just push it further into the context of memories.

As with the first step, it can be expected that this step will take about four weeks. With cognitive processing, therapists do not like to move fast. This is because they need to make sure that each step of the process is being done the correct way and that the patient has moved from one step to the next in the proper way before they can begin it. They will not be able to be successful with any of the steps if they are not able to get through the first or second step.

Getting Through It

Once someone has found the memories and accepted them, they may think that they are out of the woods and that they are healed of their anxiety and depression. This is not the case, though, and it is the point at which many people trip up and lose their own ability to be able to deal with the memories and the things that they have because of them. They need to continue to learn how to not repress memories and to keep things light for themselves. It is important to make sure that they know how to get through the situations that they are in and that they are making sure that they will not do it again.

After the cognitive processing is done, the person's brain will be trained to not repress memories and to keep themselves as levelheaded as possible in all situations. The memories that they had, even the ones they did not know about, will no longer be triggers and they will not have to worry about the different problems that come with the triggers. Cognitive processing is effective in that it promotes someone's good memories and allows them to accept the bad while not bringing them up all of the time.

It is important to note that there are many problems that can come with memory repression. This is especially true if someone has anxiety and/or depression due to sexual assault, PTSD or something similar. The memories can be painful and bring them up out of a repressed state can make things even worse for the person. That is why it is important to consult with a mental health professional before trying to do cognitive processing therapy. It can sometimes be detrimental and having the help of a professional will allow the therapy to be more successful.

Chapter 12 Reprocessing And Emdt

Some cognitive behavioral therapy methods work with the mental aspect of the brain while others work with the physical. It can sometimes be hard to cope, especially when anxiety is spiraling out of control. People need to learn how to process that and figure out a coping method that works right for them. The reprocessing therapy works by focusing on the movement of the eyes and how it is able to help a person reprocess all of the information that they have stored in their own brain depending on the different ways that things will be able to go for them and the way that things can be improved when it comes to their abilities.

History

When you are planning on using reprocessing, there are several things that you will first need to take a look at. As with all things that you do in cognitive behavioral therapy, you will need to look into the past to find the memories that can function as triggers for your anxiety and depression. You need to keep track of these memories because this is how you are going to make a change to the triggers that you have the memories that you have made in the past.

Relaxing

You can start to relax the first time that you try to do reprocessing. You will need to take time when you are not stressed about anything and notice the sensations that you feel. Relax your eye muscles, the rest of your head muscles and everything else so that you can make sure that you are getting the most out of the situation. It will allow you the chance to ensure that you are relaxed. Keep track of these feelings. You can then use this when you are having a stressful time.

Cognition Scale

The cognition scale is used to see how well you can relax while you are thinking about memory as a trigger or while there is a trigger that is present and making you tense. It is expected that you would be a 1 or a 2 on the scale when you are first getting started with reprocessing, but by the end of treatment, you should be at the highest point on the scale, a 7. This takes some time and a lot of positive imagery to be able to conquer in the way that you need to start healing.

Retraining

There are several steps to the process, but the retraining part is what you will be able to focus on the most. This is what will make things work the right way for you and will allow you the chance to make sure that you have mastered reprocessing. Once you have learned how to do this, your brain will be trained to immediately start associating the relaxation techniques with the trigger that previously made you feel anxious or upset in any way.

Strengthening

While it may seem that having your brain automatically associate good things with the stimuli you previously experienced in a negative light, this is not always the best way to be able to handle the situation. You will need to learn how to do this in a way that makes more sense and so that you can continue to strengthen the belief that you have that this is, in fact, a positive thing. Doing this will allow you to continue using this technique and will allow you to keep the anxiety at bay for years even after you have finished it.

The easiest way for you to continue strengthening your beliefs is to consistently go back to that place of relaxation. While your brain is still able to do this on its own, you will want to make sure that you do it on a cognitive level as well. You do not need to do this every time that you think that something is going wrong, but when you begin to get stressed or notice stimuli affecting you, you should try to go back to the place of relaxation. There is nothing new to learn when it comes to strengthening, but you will need to remember to practice what you have already learned.

Lingering Sensations

If there are any types of sensations that could cause a person to feel like they are going to become anxious again or that they are going to start to stress, there needs to be a plan in place to be able to handle them. This could be anything from mild stress to tension to need to be surrounded by people or anything else that could signal oncoming anxiety. When a person starts to feel this, they need to take their time and specifically relax for the benefit of themselves. This is the only way that they can get through it.

One thing that many therapists will suggest that their clients do is to go looking for these thoughts and these feelings. When they start to feel a twinge of something bad happening, they need to latch onto that and make sure that they are trying to figure out how to react to it so that they will be able to do more. They can benefit from this because they will be able to learn as much as possible about what makes it happen and what they can do to make it relax. Even years after therapy has been completed, you can benefit from seeking out lingering sensations and quashing them.

Logging It

Throughout all of the different things that go on with reprocessing, you need to log them. You should figure out what you are doing, what you feel and the sensations that you have so that you will be able to learn as much as possible about the different things that are going on. It is important to log it and keep track of it so that you can learn what your triggers are, how to relax through them and how to make sure that you are doing things the right way when you are trying to fix your anxiety and your depression.

Determination

Since you have logged all of the information, it will be easy for both you and your therapist to go back and see what made the determination on whether or not you were going to get anxious over something. You may find that simply logging the information can help with anxiety, but you will need to determine why you are anxious, what you have done to fix it and what has worked for you to be able to get through any type of situation or trigger.

The biggest aspect of reprocessing is the physical aspect. Averting your eyes to something else, allowing them to look inward at what you are doing and giving yourself a chance to notice the physical symptoms of what is happening when a trigger is brought to your attention are all ways that you can redirect your own attention away from the different aspects of your life. It is something that you will need to be able to do and use to your advantage when it comes time to continue with the reprocessing and with your own life while trying to overcome the anxiety and depression.

Chapter 13 Treatment Of Cognitive Disorders

A lot of options are available for the treatment of cognitive disorders. There are certain disorders can be completely cured but there are others that cannot. In the latter case, the treatment can help in improving the quality of life for the person as much as possible. Cognitive dysfunctions can be improved with the help of verified drugs and some supplements. There are drugs like antidepressants that help in treating associated conditions like depression or anxiety. Drugs are also used to help the person retain as much memory as possible when the condition is identified early. The therapist or doctor has to assess the patient to determine what their exact condition is and what treatment or medication will work best for them. It is also to be noted that while these drugs for cognitive disorders are helpful, they may also have certain side effects. The patient might experience dizziness and even insomnia. Doctors have to keep a check on the effect of any medicine when it is initially prescribed. If the drug does not work as intended or has too many side effects on a particular individual, the doctor will switch to another drug or treatment that might be more suitable.

Cognitive disorders are really hard for people to live with. These dysfunctions change a lot about their life and sometimes in a way that it seems like a completely different person. The person suffering needs a lot of support and the right treatment to help make things as good as possible. They often experience a lot of frustration and anger over having to face such issues in the first place. They are silent viewers of how the disease impacts their lives. It has a negative effect on their mental health and can lead to maladaptive behavior in many of these people. They try to assert control over their lives and body by doing the wrong things. This may be in the form of consuming excessive alcohol or even taking drugs.

A lot of patients try stimulating drugs because these allow them to gain a little more control for a short while. However, they usually do so without prescription and can become dependent on these drugs. This is how drug abuse may develop. A lot of these people have also lost their lives by overdosing on prescription drugs. Patients need to realize that they are not qualified to increase or even decrease the dosage of their medication without consultation from a doctor. The drugs will not work better if they just increase the dosage. Too much can, instead, have a completely opposite effect than was intended. Trying to get off this habit also causes more pain and suffering to the patient as they suffer from withdrawal symptoms. The therapist or doctor needs to supervise the consumption of these drugs for such patients. If not, it can end up being fatal. A lot of cognitive disorders are actually caused by or otherwise linked to substance abuse. For instance, alcoholics tend to be more prone to ADHD.

Cognitive Behavioral Therapy helps people with cognitive disorders or dysfunction in many ways. It improves their life even without additional medication. The therapy helps patients identify the negative thoughts and behavior they have been practicing and understand the impact of these. Cognitive Behavioral Therapy then teaches them to exercise more control and be more positive no matter what problems they face. The various phases and techniques of Cognitive Behavioral Therapy help people with cognitive issues to improve their condition to a large extent.

Cognitive distortions are basically like bad habits and they can be treated well with the help of CBT. Cognitive restructuring is an important part of this. It teaches the person to identify any of their maladaptive thoughts and to them refute them. Various Cognitive Behavioral Therapy techniques like thought recording and imagery are used for this purpose. Cognitive restricting aims to help the person change their thought patterns in a way that less stress is induced in the future or hopefully none at all. Cognitive restructuring will usually require the assistance of a therapist and is not something that can be carried out effectively by yourself.

In the end, it is important to be more aware of the symptoms of any cognitive dysfunctions if you want to maintain a good quality of life in the long term. Another helpful practice to include in your life is mindfulness meditation to help with all of this.

Age is a Factor

One important factor to consider in Cognitive Behavioral Therapy is that people may react differently to it at times and their age plays a major role in this. The same therapy will show different results in a person who is old and different in a person who is much younger. The term used to describe this phenomenon is Cohort's effect. Every therapist has to keep this impact of age in mind when opting for a particular therapy to treat a person. In Cognitive Behavioral Therapy, the client has to be willing to shed their old ways of thinking. Instead, they need to make an effort to adapt to a new and more positive way. The therapist will ask the client to make a number of changes when they undergo Cognitive Behavioral Therapy. There are certain people who will embrace these changes with open arms while others will be much more resistant to it. We have already mentioned this elsewhere in the book because it really is true. Each person will react differently to therapy and a lot of factors play a role in this. Their economic standing and social position are also factors. The therapist should keep these factors in mind when they determine a course of therapy so that the right methods are applied. If not, the therapy will not be as effective as it should. Out of these factors we mentioned, age is an important factor to consider due to a number of reasons. Some of these are as follows:

- As we grow older, we become creatures of habit. We like doing the same things that we have always done and will be less open to any change.

- Each person will have established a set of their own principles as they grow older and they stick by them no matter what.

- An older person will have a more fixed view of what is wrong and what is right.

- Age makes people close off mentally and resist any change in their life because there is comfort in routine.

- As we grow older, we take more time to adapt to anything new. This causes more stress in our lives. Such things take more time and effort than they would if we were younger.

- Older people scrutinize every single thing minutely and look for flaws. They are less trusting than a younger person.

You will realize that these are the changes that every person undergoes, as they grow older. Everyone develops a specific personality with certain values, habits, and thinking. We tend to set some limits and boundaries that we are very reluctant to cross if at all. Change does not appeal to anyone as they age.

Our physical, social and economic situation also affects how we think and makes us less willing to accommodate any recommended changes despite the good intentions of the therapist. You will notice how older people have a habit of comparing how things were different when they were young. They tend to criticize the way the youth live and do things and talk of how their ways were and are much better. They don't stop to consider that maybe the present is much better than what the past was in some ways. This difficulty in accepting change is why Cognitive Behavioral Therapy is not always easy or effective for someone who is old.

This therapy requires the client to be a willing participant to takes the initiative to act on the recommended changes at every point in the therapy. An older person will have to be willing to change how they have been thinking and heaving for years together and this is not an easy task. They will have to get rid of their opinions and prejudices just because the therapy demands it. You may know that the therapy is designed to improve things for you, in the long run, but this doesn't make it any easier to go through the process. This resistance or defiance in older people makes it difficult for therapists to carry out Cognitive Behavioral Therapy on them. This is why you have to understand that age can be a challenging factor for therapists to deal with. They have to be more careful and tackle the problem in different ways. They will have to find innovative and slightly manipulative ways to allow older people to conform to the therapy. As long as it benefits the willing participant, in the long run, it's okay.

CBT in Practice

There are numerous ways of incorporating Cognitive Behavioral Therapy in your life. These simple and practical ways can be adopted by almost everyone, and anyone can reap the benefits from them. Many different techniques and tools are used in Cognitive Behavioral Therapy, most of these are of dual-nature, and this means that they can be used as a form of therapy or they can be used in everyday life as well. Here is a small list of various common, yet effective CBT practices that you can incorporate in your life.

Journaling

Journaling is a popular method of gathering your thoughts, ideas, moods, etc. People have been journaling for a long time as a method of collecting and situating their ideas. A CBT journal is like any other journal; however, it will help you and will prove to be therapeutic. In CBT journal, you are supposed to mention different factors along with your ideas, moods, and thoughts. You are supposed to include other things such as the intensity of the thought, the extent of the thought, the source of the thought, the time and the place of the thought, and the reaction you had towards the thought. This technique will thus help you to identify your emotional tendencies and thought patterns and will help you understand, adapt, change, and cope with them.

Unraveling Cognitive Distortions

The main goal of CBT is unraveling cognitive distortions. Through CBT, you can understand whether you have cognitive problems and if yes, what kind of problems you have. To understand cognitive distortions, you first need to know what sort of distortions are common. This involves identifying and tackling harmful automatic thoughts.

Cognitive Restructuring

When you have identified distortions, you need to explore and identify the roots of these distortions. Finding the roots of the distortions is necessary, as it will help you to realize the reason why you believe them. Once you understand that a belief is bad, harmful, and destructive, you can start tackling and challenging it.

For instance, let's imagine that you are a person who is a firm believer who thinks that they need to have a high-paying job to be a respected individual in the society. Suddenly you lose this job. Now you will end up thinking low of yourself and feeling bad. This is a false belief, and instead of accepting, which will only lead to negative thoughts about yourself, use this as an opportunity to change your beliefs about respect and respectability. Consider things that you did not consider before and tackle your faulty beliefs head-on.

Exposure and Response Prevention

OCD has become a significant problem now, and many people suffer from it. This technique is often recommended for people who suffer from obsessive-compulsive disorder. In this technique you are supposed to expose yourself to a behavior that would normally trigger a compulsive behavior, however, instead of giving in to it, you are supposed to control your emotions and avoid performing the act.

This method works even better if you combine it with journaling. Through journaling, you will be able to understand how this technique makes you feel.

Interoceptive Exposure

This technique is highly recommended for people who suffer from panic attacks and anxiety. In this method, your body is exposed to sensations that you are afraid of. This is done to elicit responses through which unhelpful and fearsome beliefs attached to the sensations are activated. You are supposed to concentrate on these feelings and let the new sensations come through. Through this technique, the person is made to understand that the symptoms associated with panic are not dangerous even if they may seem uncomfortable. The discomfort may or may not go away with time.

Nightmare Exposure and Rescripting

Nightmare exposure and rescripting is another popular technique in CBT circles. It is especially recommended for people who suffer from nightmares and night terrors. This method is similar to interoceptive exposure in which the nightmare is elicited which, in turn, channels the proper emotion. Once the emotion has become significant, the therapist and the client can work together to find out the necessary emotion and then form an image that will accompany this new emotion.

Play the Script Until the End

This is another technique recommended for people suffering from fear, phobia, and anxiety. In this technique, the person who has a crippling fear or anxiety related to something is made to go through a thought experiment. In this experiment, they are asked to imagine the worst outcome of a scenario. By playing out this worst-case scenario, the individual can understand that even if their fears become a reality, their outcome will be perhaps manageable or at least they will be ready for it.

Progressive Muscle Relaxation

People who practice mindfulness must be aware of this technique already. This technique is quite similar to body scan method. In this technique, you are supposed to relax one muscle group at a time and repeat it until your whole body becomes relaxed. To help you perform this technique, you can use YouTube videos, audio guidance, etc. or if you are comfortable, you can do this with just your mind as well. This method is especially great for people who are looking to gain more focus and calm their nerves.

Relaxed Breathing

This is another method that is well known with mindfulness practitioners. In this method, you can use a variety of methods to regularize and calm your breathing. These include unguided as well as guided imagery, YouTube videos, audio clips, scripts, etc. Calming and regularizing your breathing can help you to look at your problems from different perspectives and point of views. You will be able to make a more balanced, rational, and effective decision once when you are calm and sober.

These techniques can prove to be a boon for people suffering from various afflictions such as depression, fear, anxiety, panic disorder, OCD, etc. The techniques given in this section are easy and thus can be performed with or without the help of a therapist. To make these techniques work better, make some worksheets and handouts that will help you to keep track of everything.

Conclusion

This book has provided you with essential information on the most common mental health issues, with emphasis on both anxiety and depression, and how cognitive behavioral therapy is a viable treatment option for each of the most common issues people face. It taught you how to identify negative automatic thoughts, and provided reasons for why these thoughts can be toxic to your mental wellbeing. It covered what emotional triggers are, and why we suffer from them. Cognitive behavioral therapy was discussed in depth, including what the most common misconceptions are, and what treatment commonly entails. A list of cognitive distortions were provided, along with how to identify when your thoughts may be plagued by them. Steps on breaking free from negative thoughts and cognitive distortions were provided, and lastly, the most common techniques cognitive behavioral therapy employs were discussed.

Now that you are armed with this knowledge and these tools, you are prepared to begin rewiring your thinking. Regardless of why you have decided to read this book, the tools contained within should enable you to begin the journey of cognitive restructuring. With time, effort, and perseverance, you are prepared to challenge your negative, harmful behaviors and thoughts in order to replace them with something conducive to the healthy lifestyle you strive to achieve.

Remember, just as you can get caught in a loop of negative thoughts, feelings, and behaviors, you can also get caught in a loop of positivity. A positive way of thinking will breed positive feelings, which will leave you inclined to behave in positive ways. It will take time to get to the point where the positive thinking becomes an instinctive reflex, especially if you have carried your cognitive distortions for most or all of your life, but breaking your negative habit will better nearly every aspect of your life. Remain patient as you work through the process, and understand that in a traditional cognitive behavioral therapy treatment, the process still takes three to four months to show effects. The skills in this book take time to develop and master, but like all good things, the results will absolutely be worth the wait. In times of weakness, when you feel like quitting or are feeling discouraged, remind yourself to look at how far you have come. Even just understanding what tricks your brain tries to play on you is a monumental step toward correcting your problem and is worthy of celebration. Despite how you may feel during the hard times, you are absolutely worthy of the happiness that will come from freeing your mind from the toxicity of your cognitive distortions and negative thoughts. You are worthy of fulfillment and enjoying your life. You are absolutely worth the effort it will take to better your mental health, and you deserve to know the feeling of loving who you are.

If you do engage in therapy with a skilled professional, you can expect your sessions to be short and structured. Despite the brevity, the structure maximizes the benefit to you. Typically, the beginning of the session is addressing any concerns you may have had during the time since your last session has ended, as well as reflecting on whatever assignment you were given to practice during the week. You then begin to learn a new skill that will be useful for you, followed by practicing your skills in a controlled environment with the therapist. You are then given the assignment to complete before meeting once again before you are sent on your way.

By having an assignment that requires you to use the skills taught to you during the week in real time, in real life situations, you are able to really reinforce their use in your life. As the skills taught prove themselves effective, you then use those skills more often, which gives you more benefits and positive reinforcement, which leads you to use them even more. This positive reinforcement cycle really affirms that the therapy process is working while also making waves in your life.

Just think; one tiny negative thought can derail your entire day, just like a single stone tossed into the water can ripple out to affect water quite a distance away from it. Now imagine, instead of just a pebble of a negative thought, you pick up a fistful of positive thoughts and behaviors turned into rocks and throw them into the water. It will make a much larger effect and will be much more noticeable. Those big waves are what you create as you utilize the skills taught in therapy in real time to be compliant with therapy.

This, in part, is one of the reasons CBT is so effective. You are literally tasked with changing thoughts behaviors in real time and taught the skills to do so rather than spending your time dwelling on the past to eventually try to come to terms with whatever has happened in your past. As you begin to utilize the skills and find them effective, your therapist is able to walk you through why the process worked in the first place, leaving you with a thorough understanding of how your mind works. This leaves you understanding the changes in your life at a fundamental level, which leaves you much more likely to continue including them in your life in various aspects. If you discover that repeating affirmations helped you overcome your crippling anxiety by helping you remain grounded during an exam, you may decide to try implementing them when you are stressed about a big deadline at work, or to stop yourself from lashing out at people when you are upset. Likewise, if grounding techniques worked when you felt overwhelmingly angry, you may try using them when you feel other overwhelming feelings as well. As these skills and techniques build upon themselves, they inspire you to continue making changes, and you end up with a domino effect. One change leads to another, then another and another, until you barely recognize the life you are living now but in a good way. The changes that will happen will seem almost too good to be true, but they are entirely possible if you put in the dedication.

Without a therapist to guide you, this process is a little bit different. There will not be anyone trained to help you or bounce ideas off of, nor is there anyone who can walk you through the steps and explain why things work. You have a book telling you what to do, but unable to provide real-time feedback to help you better if it is necessary. You have a cookie cutter assignment designed to help the general public, and you have to tweak it to make it specific to you and your situation. This does not mean it is impossible. However, if it were, this book would be pointless! You absolutely can attempt CBT on your own since the process itself is so relatively simple and action-based, if you have the dedication and fortitude to do so. However, if at any point, it is too much for you to handle, you should absolutely seek out professional help.

With a book, you are given an understanding of what CBT entails, as well as key concepts. You are also guided through a handful of strategies and assignments to complete that are provided. It is up to you to keep up with the work, and up to you to make sure the assignments you complete are beneficial to you. So long as you are self-driven, this process will most likely be entirely doable for you on your own. Keep in mind that there are no absolutes in psychology, however, and if you do not find this process useful, keep looking for the methods that work for you, even if that means seeking therapy, speaking to a doctor about medication, or choosing an entirely different approach altogether. Both of those are valid decisions you could make to better your situation, even if they do not involve this book.